GARLAND STUDIES IN

Entrepreneurship

STUART BRUCHEY

Allan Nevins Professor Emeritus
American Economic History
Columbia University

GENERAL EDITOR

A Garland Series

An Analysis of
Black Business Enterprises

John W. Handy

Garland Publishing, Inc.
New York & London
1989

Library of Congress Cataloging-in-Publication Data

Handy, John.
An analysis of Black business enterprises / John W. Handy.
p. cm. — (Garland studies in entrepreneurship)
ISBN 0-8240-3365-5 (alk. paper)
1. Small business—United States—Econometric models.
2. Afro-American business enterprises—Econometric models.
3. Afro-American business enterprises—Statistics.
I. Title. II. Series.
HD2346.U5H38 1989
338.7'408996073—dc20   89-36165

Printed on acid-free, 250-year-life paper

Manufactured in the United States of America

To Nia and Erin

PREFACE

Modern research on minority business development began twenty years ago -- springing from the works of Flournoy Coles, Andrew Brimmer, Theodore Cross, and Ed Irons. A debt is owed them for highlighting critical areas of concern and approaches to the study of the subject. While these earlier works have not been without criticism, they have stimulated a whole generation of researchers in the area of minority business research.

The most recent research in the field, started after 1980, has been largely encouraged and underwritten by the Minority Business Development Agency of the U.S. Department of Commerce. This body of research has sought to employ more rigorous empirical methods, carefully constructed methodology, and the use of more appropriate data. New areas of research have stressed equity capital and debt structure, role models and the social status of minority business ownership, analysis of industry trends of minority-owned firms, and alternative models of business growth.

The objective of this present study is to contribute to our current knowledge concerning the causes of firm formation and firm failure within the black-owned business sector across U.S. metropolitan areas.

An entrepreneurial model of firm formation and continuation was constructed which analyzed factors involved in choosing self-employment, (i) under conditions of certainty, (ii) under conditions of risk and uncertainty, and (iii) under conditions of discrimination. Hypotheses drawn from the theoretical model were investigated using factor analysis and ordinary least square estimation. The study incorporated, as explanatory factors, local market conditions, capital availability, business

i

human capital, and measures of opportunity costs facing potential and existing black entrepreneurs. Data measuring firm failures and firm formations were constructed from a special one-time tabulation conducted by the United States Minority Business Development Agency in 1983.

The results indicated that macro conditions were much better at predicting black-owned firm formations than firm failures. The evidence also indicated that,

1. Greater supplies of black professionals and managers working in large corporations were highly complementary to the formation of black-owned firms.

2. Black-owned commercial banks have been important in sustaining black firms, but they have not been significant in providing start-up capital for employment generating firms.

3. Small Business Administration loans to black businessmen were directly associated with black firm formation only in the western region, and were of little importance in lowering failure rates overall.

4. While higher black median family income was directly associated with the formation of small, nonemployer black firms offering personalized products and services, it was also directly related to failure rates of larger, employment generating black enterprises.

5. Metropolitan areas which initially possessed a greater probability of blacks being self-employed, continued to sustain their relative advantage in that area over time.

6. Controlling for income, greater levels of residential segregation were negatively associated with black firm formations.

7. Business formation and failure rates of larger black firms with paid employees were sensitive to general business cycle activity.

I am indebted to all my former colleagues at the Southern Center for Studies in Public Policy at Clark Atlanta University, where much of this research was completed. I would also like to thank Drs. David Sjoquist, Keith Ihlanfeldt, Bruce Seaman and Kamal El-Sheshai, who were generous with their time and knowledge during the preparation of my dissertation, which forms the basis of this publication.

TABLE OF CONTENTS

iv

LIST OF TABLES

vii

LIST OF ILLUSTRATIONS

Chapter I

INTRODUCTION

Expanding minority business ownership has been an item on the nation's social agenda for more than twenty years. The beginning of public policy concern over minority business ownership was marked by two events. The first was the establishment of the Office of Minority Business Enterprise within the Department of Commerce in 1968.[1] This marked the first time that a federal agency was given the specific charge of coordinating federal efforts to assist black and other minority businessmen. As such, it formalized as a specific aspect of federal policy the development of minority-owned businesses. Other governmental agencies including the Small Business Administration, the Economic Development Administration, and the Department of Housing and Urban Development were also given the task of helping to stimulate minority economic development from this date. The second notable event was the Conference on Black Economic Development sponsored by the Thirty-Fifth American Assembly in April, 1969 under the auspices of Columbia University. It constituted the first national conference to explore the social rationale for black economic development and alternative approaches to achieve it.[2]

The principle motivation for the interest in this area of public policy stems from the general awareness of the low rate of minority participation in the ownership of American businesses. According to Commerce Department and

Internal Revenue Service data, there was a total of about 9.8 million business enterprises in the United States in 1972 and approximately 368 thousand of these businesses were owned by minorities. Of this total, 188 thousand were owned by blacks, 116 thousand were owned by Hispanics, and 64 thousand were owned by Asian-Americans and other minorities. By 1977, the total number of business enterprises in the United States had increased to about 11.7 million and the 1977 Survey of Minority-Owned Business Enterprises indicated that the number of businesses owned by minorities had increased to 562 thousand, with blacks owning 231 thousand of these firms, Hispanics owning 219 thousand and Asian-Americans and others owning the remaining 112 thousand firms. By 1982, African-Americans owned 339 thousand firms, Hispanics 248 thousand firms, and Asian-Americans 256 thousand firms out of the 14.5 million firms in the United States.[3] The proportion of American business enterprises owned by blacks, therefore, grew from 2.0 percent in 1972 and 1977 to 2.3 percent in 1982. The proportion of firms owned by Hispanics went from 1.2 percent in 1972 to 1.9 percent in 1977 and 1.7 percent in 1982, while the proportion owned by Asian-Americans and others has increased from 0.6 percent 1972 and 0.9 percent in 1977 to 1.8 percent of all firms in 1982. To further place these estimates in perspective, we note that from 1977 to 1982 the proportion of businesses owned by blacks has remained at about one-sixth of the proportion of blacks in the American population, while the proportion of businesses owned by Hispanics has fallen from one-third to one-quarter of their population proportion; and the proportion of American businesses owned by Asian-Americans has increased from 43 percent to 56 percent of their population proportion.

The disparity in minority participation in American business is even more vividly revealed by the discrepancy between the total receipts of minority firms and all U.S. firms. In 1972, minority firms had gross receipts of about 13.65 billion dollars, while the gross receipts of all firms totaled 2.32 trillion dollars. By 1977, the receipts of minority firms had increased to 26.4 billion dollars while the receipts of all firms were about 4.7 trillion dollars. By 1982, the figures were 45.3 billion and 6.9 trillion dollars respectively. Thus, while there was a slight increase in the share of receipts going to minority owned businesses since 1972, the proportion of total receipts received by all minority firms has remained consistently between .60 and .65 of one percent from 1972 to 1982. Moreover, the share of receipts received by minority-owned businesses has remained at about three percent of the proportion of minorities in the population. From 1972 to 1977, the share of receipts received by black-owned businesses (0.2 of one percent) was less than two percent of the proportion of blacks in the population and less than 1.5 percent of the proportion of blacks in the population in 1982.

Since the mid-1960s, federal policymakers have been engaged in an effort to develop strategies that would improve the rate and nature of minority participation in the ownership of American business. A variety of policies have been developed including: financial support (through grants, loan guarantees and direct loans), technical support, and marketing support (through federal procurement and other government set-aside programs). However, there has been an increasing awareness that despite these efforts, systematic investigation of minority firm behavior has been a largely neglected area of research:

> The goal of federal assistance to minority and women-owned businesses is to encourage their formation, growth and survival, so that they may face obstacles no different than those of the general business community. Progress toward this end must be measured through research which will monitor the changing status of the targeted groups. Although interest has increased substantially in the progress and problems of minority and women-owned businesses, assessment[4] of these areas has been hindered by a lack of current and appropriate data.

3

A data base developed in 1983 by the Minority Business Development Agency (MBDA) of the Department of Commerce sought for the first time to address some of the deficiencies in minority-business research. The data base, called the Matched and Unmatched Minority - Owned Business Records 1972/1977 by Standard Metropolitan Statistical Areas, was derived from the Census Bureau's micro data files originally used in producing the 1972 and 1977 Survey of Minority-Owned Business Enterprise. While the original published versions of the 1972 and 1977 Survey included statistics on number of firms, total employment, gross receipts, and annual payroll across several geographic, industrial and size categories, they could not yield any insight into the dynamic process of firm formation and failure. The 1983 MBDA Matched and Unmatched Minority-Owned Business Records data base, on the other hand, was designed specifically, according to the chief of the Research Division of MBDA, "to test hypotheses about relative business formation and failure rates between minority and nonminority-owned businesses. Those hypotheses have not yet been tested because comparable data on the nonminority groups is not available."[5]

THE PROBLEM TO BE STUDIED

This present study undertakes the task of increasing our understanding of the determinants of business participation, firm formation and firm failure within the black business sector itself. The principal objective of this work is to contribute to our current knowledge about the causes of variation across metropolitan areas in the rates of formation, failure and expansion of black-owned businesses at the one-digit SIC level.

While previous research has raised a number of hypotheses about the potential for expanding the black-owned business sector, limitations in available

4

data and research methodology have resulted in less than convincing empirical evidence. Changes over time, both in the business sector itself and in the impact of surrounding and community economic conditions, have been largely absent, even in many of the better studies on black and minority development. The earliest studies were simply speculative -- containing little or no empirical investigations to test the link between the postualed causal factors and overall performance of the black business sector. Thus, much of the speculative and theoretical analyses has not been well tested.

This study focuses on the black-owned business sector. While it is expected that the findings of the study will be useful in understanding growth and change for minority-owned businesses in general, differences in both the historical circumstances and current situation of the different minority groups make group-specific analyses mandatory. Moreover, the study of black-owned businesses is in many ways the most perplexing. While black-owned businesses represent the largest proportion of minority-owned businesses (41 percent), they rank last in business receipts per firm ($37,000 versus $70,000 for Asians and $60,400 for Hispanics)[6], and last among the three racial/ethnic groups in the likelihood of selecting business ownership as a livelihood. While 6.4 percent of the general population are business owners, 1.3 percent of blacks are entrepreneurs compared to 5.5 percent of Asians and 1.7 percent of Hispanics.

This study represents one of the first attempts to do a rigorous empirical analysis of the overall business performance of a particular minority group, specifically that of black-owned businesses in standard metropolitan statistical areas.[7] The analysis incorporates many of the factors identified by our theoretical model and in the previous literature as being important determinants of the variation in formation and failure rates of black-owned business enterprises. A primary concern of the research is the establishment of proper test procedures to study the pattern of variation in business performance of the local black business sector nationwide and by industry classification. The study takes a decidely macro approach and concentrates on determining the impact of a variety of macro factors on the overall change in black business ownership as measured by formation, failure, and continuation rates.

This study, therefore, will incorporate SMSA-specific macro factors concerning local economic market conditions, capital access, business human capital, area-wide opportunity costs, and state-of-nature risk, as explantory factors, onto a set of complete count data of 187,602 black-owned firms in 1972 and 231,000 black-owned firms in 1977. Since this data comprises a complete count of black-owned firms, it avoids the response and selectivity bias prevalent in earlier work.

SIGNIFICANCE OF THE PROBLEM

While the argument may be advanced that the problems of minority businesses are not different than the problems of small businesses in general, there are at least four reasons to differentiate between these two groups of business enterprises. The first, as we have already outlined, lies in the fact that minority business are underrepresented in small business ownership by all measures of participation rates and receipt shares in every industry. Second, as shown by Bates and Furino,[8] minority business enterprises are more dependent on long-term capital debt than are similarly sized non-minority businesses which have greater access to short-term financing and equity capital. This implies a much greater sensitivity to cyclical fluctuations on the part of minority business than for small businesses overall. Third, minority-owned business enterprises are on the average 30 percent more labor intensive than are small businesses in general. And last, minority-owned businesses are concentrated in the central cities where the majority of the various minority populations reside.   Hence, minority businesses are located precisely in those areas where employment and community development needs are most urgent.

Consistent with this last observation, the importance of this study stems from the importance of business development in providing greater economic and employment opportunities, and in helping to raise the standard of living of many ethnic communities. This is not a normative judgement, but simply a historical fact. This study, of course, does not in any way diminish the place and importance of the larger business community where the clear majority of all ethnic and racial groups work and earn income. However, it is quite significant that the 100 largest black-owned companies in 1977 generated altogether only $870 million in receipts which would have collectively placed them below the 250th individual business on the Fortune 500 industrial list. Certainly, no identifiable community, regardless of the racial, sexual or ethnic identification scheme used, can be considered an integral part of American business ownership when it constitutes 12 percent of the population but only 2.0 percent of the business-owning class, and less than .2 of one percent of all business receipts.

Despite the modest success of federal government efforts to date, it is likely that private sector business development strategies will have to play a larger role in future efforts to improve the position of minorities in the United States. First, during the past two decades, substantial sums were expended on public strategies to improve the economic position of minorities which, arguably, produced limited

7

results and increased minority dependency on government programs. Second, the mood in public policy has shifted and now places increased emphasis on private sector solutions. However, if a new business development strategy is to be successfully developed and accepted by the public, poliymakers will require much better information than they currently have concerning the quantitiative aspects of various causes, solutions, and impacts.

METHODOLOGY

The general conceptual framework of this thesis stems from two contentions: The first is that the role of the minority entrepreneur is central to minority business formation and growth. The successful entrepreneur must display special aptitudes for bearing risk and uncertainty which permit him to act as a catalytic agent and promoter for new investment and production opportunities. The second contention is that the choice of entrepreneurial livelihood and the probability of small firm failure or success must be understood as an outgrowth of the opportunity costs involved in undertaking such an enterprise, and of the ability of the entrepreneur - owner to reinvest retained earnings for survival and growth of the firm. In turn, these factors should be viewed within the context of a risky economic environment within which these firms must potentially or actually operate. The level or degree of risk in different locations is influenced both by macro economic conditions that impact all businesses (which we define as state-of-nature risk factors) and the problems and circumstances more unique to the black community. The influence of these special factors will often mediate to some degree the impact of general economic forces determining the distribution of opportunities for business development.

With these considerations, a model is developed in three stages which outlines (1) the factors involved in choosing self-employment under conditions of certainty, and the importance of these factors on firm formation, likelihood of continuance, and employment size of firm; (2) the impact of private relative risk aversion and economy-wide risk under uncertainty on the entrepreneurial decision; and (3) the impact of discrimination on the efficiency, and the likelihood of entry and continuation of black-owned firms.

Several hypotheses emerge from these theoretical considerations which are investigated using a combination of factor analysis and ordinary least square estimation. The criterion variables include number of new firm formations and number of business failures between 1972 and 1977 by geographical location. Firm formations are measured per 1,000 black population to correct for heteroscedasticity stemming from the varying sizes among standard metropolitan statistical areas. Heteroscedasticity is also minimized for firm failure rates, which are measured as the ratio of failed black firms to the total number of black-owned firms in the initial period. Firm failures could not be measured in per capita terms since greater number of firms per capita, by itself, implies greater number of failures per capita. On the other hand, firm formations were measured in per capita terms, and not as a ratio to total firms, because some industries in several metropolitan areas had no firms existing in 1972, but had firms form in those industries subsequently. In addition, all such measures are grouped by firms with paid employees and by firms without employees to help capture the different impacts of firm employment size on the probability of black business formation, continuation and failure.

9

LIMITATIONS

Although this study employs an improved data source which for the first time permits an investigation of failures and formations on the total number of black-owned businesses, it too has significant limitations stemming from the nature of available data. The most serious constraint concerns the paucity of data regarding government procurement and set-asides which have clearly been important for minority-owned businesses. Federal prime contract awards to minority businesses of over $10,000 amounted to $2.65 billion in 1982.[9] This data while available by states is not available by metropolitan areas. A second major limitation is that the analysis presented here had to limited to the 1972 to 1977 period since the 1983 MBDA Survey of Matched and Unmatched Minority-Owned Business Records 1972/1977 by Standard Metropolitan Statistical Areas, is the only complete count of minority-owned firm failures and formations to have ever been undertaken. A third problem, which was referred to previously, is the lack of comparable information on formations and failures for non-minority businesses. As such, no direct comparison between minority and non-minority firm formations and failures is possible. There are also problems with government disclosure rules in the MBDA data set which result in certain industries in certain SMSAs being dropped as missing cases. This is not considered a damaging problem, however, since the resulting sample is still quite representatve and the sample size is quite adequate in every test. In addition, the differences between firms with paid employees and firms with no paid employees probably underestimates the real differences between the two sets of firms since finer breakdowns isolating the largest employment firms were not possible due to disclosure problems. Furthermore, there is a great need for the Census Bureau to separate business and professional services from personal services. It is quite clear that janitorial and household services should not be lumped with accounting, legal and medical services. The 1983 MBDA data base, unfortunately, does not make this distinction.

Despite these limitations, however, the present study represents a distinct advance in minority business research.

In Chapter II we will discuss the descriptive statistics concerning minority business participation, formation, and failure rates; and the black-owned business sector in terms of total firms, receipts, and firm size by SMSA distribution and regional location. In Chapter III we will review the minority business literature specifically as it relates to the problems of black-owned business enterprise. Chapter IV will outline the theoretical framework of entrepreneurial choice under risk and uncertainty, and the opportunity costs implications of choosing between self-employment and alternative employment. Chapter V will outline the empirical methodology, hypothesized relationships and predictions, and sources of data. Empirical results concerning black-owned business formation and failure by industry and employment status will be discussed in Chapter VI. A discussion of policy implications and recommendations is offered in the seventh and final chapter.

Chapter II

DESCRIPTIVE STATISTICS

BUSINESS PARTICIPATION, FORMATION, AND FAILURE

Rates of Business Participation by Race/Ethnic Group, and Industry

There are approximately 64 nonminority businesses for every 1,000 persons in the nonminority population, but the comparable statistic for all minorities is a participation rate of only 18 per 1,000 minority persons. When disaggregated by minority groups, the participation rate for blacks is 13 per 1,000 black population, while for Hispanic and Asian-Americans, it is 17 and 55 per 1,000 persons respectively.[1] Since the number of firms in existence must always be the cumulative number of firms formed over time net the number that have failed, the business participation rates across minority groups would lead us to expect that the gap between firm formation and failure rates would be greatest for Asian-Americans, followed by Hispanics and blacks.[2] While Table 2.1 does, in fact, reflect this, interestingly, failure rates among the three groups are very much nearer one another than formation rates. In fact, while the formation rates are statistically different from one another, failure rates among the three groups are not significantly different.

TABLE 2.1

Formations and Failures by Race/Ethnic Groups

	Firm Formations 1972-77	Firm Failures 1972-77	Number of Firms in 1972	Formation Rate	Failure Rate
All Minorities	280,165	214,238	336,997	16.6	12.7
Black	140,109	115,643	187,602	14.9	12.3
Hispanic	70,791	57,422	82,546	17.2	13.9
Asian	69,265	41,173	66,849	20.7	12.3

SOURCE: Computed from the MBDA volumes of Matched and Unmatched Firms 1972, 1977 (4 volumes), U.S. Bureau of the Census and U.S. Dept. of Commerce, 1983.

NOTE: Formation (failure) rates were computed by dividing the number of formations (failures) between 1972 and 1977 by the number of firms in the base year (1972). These rates were then divided by five to obtain an annual average rate.

Thus, one analogue for the observed greater participation rates of Hispanics and Asians in business-ownership is their choosing to form businesses at greater rates than blacks. Any analysis of possible growth and change in the black-owned business sector should, therefore, incorporate factors that may influence or discourage blacks in choosing to become entrepreneurs at the outset.

In addition, the data strongly suggests that rate of participation of minority groups in the ownership of American businesses varies markedly by industry group. Taking the ratio of minority firms per 1,000 of minority population to total small firms owned per 1,000 of total population shows the relative rate of participation of minority groups in firm ownership. For the purpose of understanding the chart below, if minority groups owned firms at the same rate as the general population, we would assign a value of 100. As can be seen from Table 2.2, all minorities are substantially underrepresented in the ownership of firms in every major

13

industry group. However, among all groups, black participation in firm ownership is lowest in every sector except transportation. Blacks tend to be most underrepresented as owners of wholesale trade; finance, insurance and real estate; and manufacturing businesses. Blacks' highest rates of participation are in the lines of transportation, service, and retail trade establishments where black businesses have traditionally been located.

TABLE 2.2

Relative Rates of Participation In Firm Ownership By Industry

	Blacks	Spanish Origin	Asian American, American Indians & Others
All Firms	13.52	35.32	41.67
Construction	14.21	40.89	18.33
Manufacturing	7.49	22.26	30.00
Transportation and Public Utilities	41.00	42.80	31.11
Wholesale Trade	3.36	14.20	28.33
Retail Trade	19.38	45.11	76.67
Finance Insurance and Real Estate	4.65	13.24	18.89
Services	21.62	41.27	62.22
All Others	3.36	7.87	20.56

SOURCE: Computed from the 3 volumes comprising the 1977 SURVEY OF MINORITY-OWNED BUSINESS ENTERPRISES (1) Black, (2) Spanish, (3)Asian Americans, American Indians and Others, Table 1 of each volume; also Sole Proprietorship Returns, the U.S. Department of Treasury, Internal Revenue Service, 1978; and also The State of Small Business, March 1983, Table 6.4, p. 144.

NOTE: Figures in Table 2.2 were computed by taking the ratio of number of minority firms in each industry to total minority population and then dividing by the ratio of total small firms in each industry to total population. The results for each industry were then multiplied by 100.

Table 2.3 displays an alternative measure of minority participation in industry by showing the relative share of receipts going to minorities. The receipts data provide an even clearer indication of the low level of minority participation in the various industries. For blacks there is not a single industry for which their participation is as great as four percent of what it would be if they participated in the same proportion that they are represented in the American populace. Although participation rates are significantly higher for the other minority classifications, the rates are still generally under 10 percent for all industries with three exceptions: Asian-Americans in services and retail trade, and Hispanics in services. The lowest three industries in terms of participation by receipts for all groups are, in order, manufacturing, transportation and public utilities, and wholesale trade. The highest industries in terms of participation by receipts are services, retail trade, and construction.

TABLE 2.3
Relative Participation in Total Small Business Receipts By Industry

	Blacks	Spanish Origin	Asian American, American Indians & Others
All Firms	1.70	4.61	9.44
Construction	2.76	9.98	8.89
Manufacturing	.34	.96	1.67
Transportation and Public Utilities	1.29	2.30	2.78
Wholesale Trade	.86	2.30	5.00
Retail Trade	3.88	9.78	26.11
Finance Insurance and Real Estate	2.07	2.88	6.11
Services	3.61	17.70	33.89
All Others	.86	3.07	5.56

SOURCE: See Table 2.2

NOTE: These figures were computed by taking the ratio of minority-owned business receipts per capita to total small business receipts per capita for each industry.

Traditionally minority-owned businesses have been participating most notably in several lines of small scale retail and service-business activity that offer minimal potential for growth. Several previous studies have indicated that incentives necessary to attract talented members of minority groups into entrepreneurial pursuit are lacking in these traditional areas of operation.[3] While the history of black businesses suggests that the limited performance of this sector has been shaped by limited access to credit and capital, limitations on educational and training opportunities, and society's attitudes about the roles that minorities should assume[4], better educated members of minority groups have, until fairly recently, shunned the business world. It is well known, for instance, that the overwhelming majority of the black middle class has historically been employed in government, teaching, high-wage blue-collar jobs, the military, and church service.[5]

Recent research, however, has indicated that over the past twenty-years minority-owned businesses have begun to diversify and expand in response to an influx of talent and capital.[6] Increased opportunities created by set-asides, preferential government policies, and loan programs have induced better educated, younger minority entrepreneurs to create and expand firms in areas such as contracting, wholesaling and manufacturing. While the traditional minority business community still consists largely of small firms serving a low-income clientele, considerably larger firms have begun to emerge that are more oriented toward a corporate and government clientele. Improved opportunities and thus shifting in the composition of minority entrepreneurship are reflected in the following facts:

(i)   nonwhite self-employed workers increased 43 percent from 1972 to 1982 compared to a 35 percent increase in white self-employed workers,[7]

(ii)   the average minority entrepreneur in 1980 was younger, better educated, and earned more than his 1960 counterpart,[8]

(iii)   on separating services into its components, we find that while 30 percent of minority entrepreneurs were in personal services and 25 percent in retail trade in 1960, by 1980 13 percent were in personal services and 22 percent in retail trade,[9]

(iv)   the percentage of minority entreprenuers in nontraditional areas of business services, finance insurance and real estate, transportation, and wholesale trade doubled from 10 percent to 20 percentage from 1960 to 1980.[10]

(v)   the minority firms in the MBDA- Dun and Bradstreet data file, representing the larger, more credit worthy firms in emerging lines of manufacturing, wholesale, and construction earned higher returns on a owner's equity than similarly sized nonminority firms.[11]

Despite these important but modest shifts, however, it is clear that existing minority-owned businesses are relatively few in number and disproportionately concentrated in certain industries. Minority groups have clearly had less success in becoming owners of business in some industries than in others, though this is beginning to change. Moreover, the industry distribution which exists appears to be skewed away from those industries that offer the highest returns to ownership.

Formation and Failure Rates by Region and Size

The most striking result from investigating formation and failure rates by region is that there is not a great difference between regions concerning minority-owned business formation and failure rates. The Pacific area of the West composed of SMSAs in California and Washington, most particularly, had the highest formation rates; while in the South the South Atlantic states of Virginia, Maryland, Georgia, North Carolina, South Carolina, and Florida had SMSAs with the lowest failure rates. Within the Northeast region SMSAs in the New England area appear to be relatively disadvantageous to minority business participation, with the lowest formation rate and highest failure rate of all the regional areas. Again, we note that the variation in formation rates is greater than for failure rates. Formation rates varied from 14.2 percent annually to 18.6 percent annually by geographical location, while failure rates only ranged from 12.0 to 14.0 percent.

TABLE 2.4

Formation and Failure Rates By Census Region

	Census Region	Formation Rate	Failure Rate
North East	New England	14.2	14.0
	Middle Atlantic	16.5	13.4
North Central	East North Central	14.7	13.0
	West North Central	17.4	13.0
South	South Atlantic	16.3	12.0
	East South Central	15.0	12.3
	West South Central	16.0	12.6
West	Mountain	15.0	13.6
	Pacific	18.6	12.7
	United States	16.6	12.7

SOURCE: Richard Stevens. "Measuring Minority Business Formation and Failure," Minority Business Development Agency, U.S. Department of Commerce, December, 1983, p. 12.

Consistent with the findings of Birch and McCracken,[12] Richard Stevens found that minority-owned firms which reach a size of over 100 employees have a significantly better chance of survival than do firms of smaller employment size.[13] In table 2.5, the six categories of group size below 100 employees had comparable rates of failure ranging from 12.0 to 12.9 percent annually. But the rate of failure for firms with 100 or more employees dropped to 9.4 percent annually.

TABLE 2.5

Minority-Owned Firm Failure Rates by Employee Size

Size Group	Failure Rate	1972 Base
Nonemployers	12.7	279,661
1-4 Employees	12.8	38,041
5-9	12.6	11,221
10-19	12.8	5,206
20-49	12.9	2,312
50-99	12.0	381
100+	9.4	175

SOURCE: Stevens, op. cit., p. 19.

Failure and Formation Rates of Black-Owned Businesses by Industry

On inspecting failure and formation rates of black-owned businesses by industry classification, a number of findings emerge. First, failure rates are clearly lower for firms with paid employees than for firms with no employees. Table 2.6 shows that the highest failure rates are found in wholesale, retail; and finance, insurance and real estate. The lowest rates of failure are in the services and transportation sectors. On inspecting the coefficient of variation,[14] however, it is also clear that within each industry failure rates for firms with paid employees vary more across metropolitan areas than do failure rates for smaller firms without paid employees; but neither appears to vary very widely especially when compared to variation in rates of formation.

One is also struck by the very large volatility of formation rates across metropolitan areas, both within industry classifications and across industries. With the exception of service firms without employees, the coefficient of variation of formation rates within each industry, regardless of employment status, is 1.5 to 3.0 times that of failure rates. There is also greater variation in formation of larger firms with paid employees than for smaller firms with no employees. With the exception of the services sector, variablity in formation rates for firms with paid employees range from 1.7 to 2.4 times that of firms without paid employees. Moreover, the range in formation rates across industries is greater than the range in failure rates. Formation rates across industries range from 10.1 to 25.0 for firms with paid employees, and from 13.4 to 21.0 for firms with no paid employees. The corresponding ranges for failures rates are only 9.2 to 13.5 for larger black firms with employees, and 10.8 to 14.4 for smaller black firms with no employees.

TABLE 2.6

Failure and Formation Rates of Black-Owned Businesses by Industry

	Failure Rate		Formation Rate	
	With Employees	Without Employees	With Employees	Without Employees
Construction	10.8 (.46)	12.5(.19)	18.6(1.08)	13.9(.44)
Manufacturing	10.5(.69)	12.9(.44)	11.2(1.54)	13.4(.84)
Transportation	9.2(.66)	11.8(.22)	14.9(1.00)	13.8(.54)
Wholesale	13.5(.56)	14.4(.39)	10.1(1.67)	16.9(.93)
Retail	11.9(.26)	14.0(.11)	14.5(.58)	13.6(.30)
Finance, Ins. Real.	12.3(.50)	13.0(.31)	10.3(1.41)	21.0(.85)
Services Ind.	10.3(.31)	10.8(.13)	25.0(.36)	18.0(.26)

SOURCE: Computed from MBDA volumes of Matched and Unmatched Firms, op. cit.

NOTE: The coefficient of variation across metropolitan areas for each industry by employment status is given in parentheses.

THE BLACK-OWNED BUSINESS SECTOR: TOTAL FIRMS, RECEIPTS, AND FIRM SCALE

Black-Owned Firms Per 1000 Black Population

Although the overall level of black business ownership is limited, there is wide variation in the level of ownership among the 155 SMSAs examined. While the mean number of black firms per thousand population in 1972 was 8.5, the range of black firms per thousand black population varied from a low of 4.2 to a high of 18.0. In 1977, the range of black firms per 1000 black population across metropolitan areas went from a low of 5.1 to a high of 30.0 with the mean number of black black firms per 1000 at 9.9. The distribution of SMSA's by number of black firms per 1000 black population for 1972 and 1977 is shown below.

TABLE 2.7

Distribution of Black Firms Across SMSAs, 1972 and 1977

Firms/1000 persons, 1972	Numbers of SMSA's	Percent of SMSA's
Less than 6	19	12.3
6 to 8	56	36.1
8 to 10	48	31.0
10 to 12	19	12.3
12 to 14	8	5.2
14 +	5	3.2
Total	155	100
Firms/1000 persons, 1977	Numbers of SMSA's	Percent of SMSA's
Less than 7	20	12.9
7 to 10	72	46.5
10 to 12	29	18.7
12 to 14	20	12.9
14 +	14	9.0
Total	155	100

In 1972 approximately 80 percent of all SMSAs in our study had 10 or fewer black businesses per 1000 black population, whereas by 1977 a little less than 60 percent of all SMSAs had 10 or fewer black businesses.

A more important point for our purposes, however, is the fact that there was also wide variation in the rate of growth in the number of firms among these SMSAs between 1972 and 1977. Growth in number of firms per 1000 population shown in the table below indicates that 12.3 percent of the SMSAs had negative or zero growth in number of firms. In all, nearly 77 percent of the SMSAs had 2 or fewer net new firms formed per 1000 population, with 23.2 percent forming more than 2 new firms per 1000 population, and nearly 6 percent forming more than 4 new firms per 1000 population. The range of increase in the number of firms per 1000 varied from -3.0 to 12.

TABLE 2.8

Growth of Black-Owned Firms Across SMSAs, 1972-1977

Growth in Firms/ 1000 persons	Numbers of SMSAs	Percent of SMSAs
Less than 0	19	12.3
0 to 1	55	35.5
1 to 2	45	29.0
2 to 3	21	13.5
3 to 4	6	3.9
4 +	9	5.8
Total	155	100

When firm growth was broken down by region, as shown in Table 2.9, we found significant regional differences in growth. The Chi-Square statistic is 60.85, which shows a systematic relation between SMSA regional location and growth in firms per 1000 Black population. This implies that a regional dummy should be included in explaining firm growth.

The West contained two-thirds of all the SMSAs having growth greater than 4.0 net new firms per 1000 despite the fact that only 13 percent of the SMSAs in our sample are located in the West. While containing nearly half of all the SMSAs in our sample, the South had no SMSAs with a firm growth of over 4.0 per 1000 population. The Midwest had 22 percent of the SMSAs in this highest firm growth category; while the Northeast had nearly 17 percent of all SMSAs and 11 percent of the SMSAs in the highest firm growth category.

At the other end of the distribution, only 5 percent of the SMSAs in the West had zero or negative firm change per capita compared to 15.4 percent of the SMSAs in the Northeast, 14.7 percent of the SMSAs in the Midwest and 12 percent of the SMSAs in the South. Moreover, only 10 percent of the SMSAs in the West had 1.0 or fewer net new firms formed per 1000 population compared to nearly 58 percent of the SMSAs in the Northeast, 59 percent in the Midwest, and nearly half of the SMSAs in the South. Thus the West is clearly the region in which the most significant net new firm formation occurred during the period of this study.

TABLE 2-9

GROWTH IN FIRMS PER 1000 BLACK POPULATION IN SMSA's
BY REGION

TABLE 2-9

	Neg. to Zero	0 - 1	1 - 2	2 - 3	3 - 4	4 and Over	SMSA's In Region as % of All SMSA's
Northeast (N = 26)							
Percent of SMSA's in NE Region	15.4	42.3	34.6	3.8	0.0	3.8	
Percent of all SMSA's across all Regions	21.1	20.0	20.0	4.8	0.0	11.1	16.8
North Central (N = 34)							
Percent of SMSA's in NC Region	14.7	44.1	14.7	11.8	8.8	5.9	
Percent of all SMSA's across all Regions	26.3	27.3	11.1	19.0	50.0	22.2	21.9
South (N = 75)							
Percent of SMSA's in South	12.0	37.3	38.7	9.3	2.7	0.0	
Percent of all SMSA's across all Regions	47.4	50.9	64.4	33.3	33.3	0.0	48.4
West (N = 20)							
Percent of SMSA's in West	5.0	5.0	10.0	45.0	5.0	30.0	
Percent of all SMSA's in all Regions	5.3	1.8	4.4	42.9	16.7	66.7	12.9

$X^2 = 60.85$ (15 degrees of freedom)

Receipts Per Capita

The variation in receipts per capita of black businesses was also fairly large. Per capita receipts in nominal terms ranged from $48 to $917 in 1972, and from $93 to $1775 in 1977. The mean amount of receipts or gross sales per capita was $246 and $344 in 1972 and 1977 respectively. More importantly for purposes of our study, these was also a wide range of growth rates in per capita receipts. The range of growth in per capita receipts between 1972 and 1977 was from -$390 to $858. The distribution of SMSAs by change in per capita sales shows that over 14 percent, or 20 out of the 139 SMSAs for which there were no missing cases, generated growth in receipts of over $200 per Black person, and nearly 14 percent, or 19 out of 139, had zero or negative growth in receipts per capita. Over 70 percent of the metropolitan areas covered showed at least moderate change. In all, about 62 out of the 139 SMSAs, or nearly 45 percent of the total SMSAs, had increases in per capita receipts which equaled or exceeded the rate of inflation of 45 percent between 1972 and 1977.

TABLE 2.10

Growth in Receipts Per Capita of Black-Owned Firms, 1972-1977

Growth in Sales/Capita ($)	Number	Percent of SMSAs Adjusted for Missing Cases	Relative to Total
Less than 0	19	13.7	12.3
0 to 100	68	48.9	43.9
100 to 200	32	23.0	20.6
200 to 300	10	7.2	6.5
300 to 400	1	0.7	0.6
400 +	9	6.5	5.8
Missing Cases	16	-	10.3
Total	155		100

Growth in per capita sales by SMSA regional location also showed that a systematic relationship exists between regional location and sales growth. The Chi-Square statistic equal to 28.7 is significant at the .02 level. Thus regional dummies are warranted in the sales growth equation also.

Table 2.11 shows that, again, the West dominated the highest growth category in terms of receipts per capita. Fifty-six percent of the total SMSAs in the highest growth category ($400 and over) were located in the West though that region only contained 14.4 percent of the SMSAs investigated. In addition, one-quarter of all the SMSAs located in the West had sales growth which placed them in the highest category. The South had only 3 percent of its SMSAs in the highest growth category and 22 percent of all SMSAs in this category although it contained 45 percent of all SMSAs in our sample. The Northeast and Midwest both had 11 percent of all the SMSAs in the highest sales growth category while containing 25 percent and 22 percent respectively of all SMSAs in our sample. Though the West had one-quarter of all its SMSAs in the highest growth category, neither the South, Northeast or Midwest had more than 4 percent of their SMSAs in the highest category. Nearly half (47.4 percent) of all SMSAs having zero or negative sales growth were in the South. In addition, while 92 percent of all the SMSAs in both the South and Northeast had sales growth under $200 per capita, only 84 perent of the Midwest SMSAs and 60 percent of Western SMSAs were in this category.

TABLE 2-11

GROWTH IN SALES PER CAPITA IN SMSA's BY REGION
($ PER CAPITA)

TABLE 2-11

	Neg. to Zero	0 - 100	100 - 200	200 - 300	300 - 400	400 and Over	Percent of All SMSA's
Northeast (N = 25)							
Percent of SMSA's in NE Region	8.0	64.0	20.0	4.0	0.0	4.0	
Percent of all SMSA's across all Regions	10.5	23.5	15.6	10.0	0.0	11.1	18.0
North Central (N = 31)							
Percent of SMSA's in NC Region	19.4	35.5	29.0	12.9	0.0	3.2	
Percent of all SMSA's across all Regions	31.6	16.2	28.1	40.0	0.0	11.1	22.3
South (N = 63)							
Percent of SMSA's in South	14.3	57.1	20.6	4.8	0.0	3.2	
Percent of all SMSA's across all Regions	47.4	52.9	40.6	30.0	0.0	22.2	45.3
West (N = 20)							
Percent of SMSA's in West	10.0	25.0	25.0	10.0	5.0	25.0	
Percent of all SMSA's in all Regions	10.5	7.4	15.6	20.0	100.0	55.6	14.4

χ^2 = 28.67   (15 degrees of freedom)

<u>Firm Scale</u>

Growth in firm scale or average sales per firm by standard metropolitan statistical areas shows that in about one-quarter of all SMSAs there was zero or negative growth in average sales per firm, with approximately one-quarter of all SMSAs exhibiting a growth in firm scale of over $10,000. This rather modest change over a five year period indicates the relative difficulty in increasing the average scale of enterprises in the black business community as compared to simply starting new business.

TABLE 2.12

Growth in Black Firm Scale Across SMSAs, 1972-1977

Growth in Sales/Firm ($)	Number of SMSAs	Percent of Total SMSAs	
		Adjusted for Missing Cases	Relative to Total
Less than 0	37	26.6	23.9
0 to 4,000	23	16.5	14.8
4,000 to 10,000	42	30.2	27.1
10,000 to 16,000	21	15.1	13.5
16,000 +	16	11.5	10.3
Missing Cases	16	-	10.3
Total	155		

Table 2.13 indicates that the growth in scale is not statistically differentiable by region as in the case of sales and firm change. That is, no systematic relationship exists between region and scale growth since Chi-Square equal to 10.6 is significant only at the .57 level. This is reflected, for instance, in the fact that while 30 percent of the West's SMSAs had an average scale increase of greater than $10,000, 28 percent of the SMSAs in the Northeast, 32.3 percent of the SMSAs in

the Midwest, and 22 percent of the SMSAs in the South also had such inreases. Only among the largest scale growth categories are differences noteworthy: One-quarter of all SMSAs in the West had scale growth in excess of $16,000 per firm compared to 4 percent of the Northeast, 11 percent of South, and 13 percent of the Midwest.

TABLE 2-13

CHANGE IN FIRM SCALE IN SMSA's BY REGION

($ Thou Per Firm)

TABLE 2-13

	Neg. to Zero	0 - 4.0	4.0 - 10.0	10.0 - 16.0	16 and Over	SMSA's In Region as % of All SMSA's
Northeast (N = 25)						
Percent of SMSA's in NE Region	16.0	20.0	36.0	24.0	4.0	
Percent of all SMSA's across all Regions	10.8	21.7	21.4	28.6	6.3	18.0
North Central (N = 31)						
Percent of SMSA's in NC Region	35.5	6.5	25.8	19.4	12.9	
Percent of all SMSA's across all Regions	29.7	8.7	19.0	28.6	25.0	22.3
South (N = 63)						
Percent of SMSA's in South	28.6	19.0	30.2	11.1	11.1	
Percent of all SMSA's across all Regions	48.6	52.2	45.2	33.3	43.8	45.3
West (N = 20)						
Percent of SMSA's in West	20.0	20.0	30.0	10.0	20.0	
Percent of all SMSA's in all Regions	10.8	17.4	14.3	9.5	25.0	14.4

χ^2 = 10.57   (12 degrees of freedom)

VARIATION IN SBA ACTIVITY AND BLACK MEDIAN FAMILY INCOME

Two other variables were found to differ by SMSA-regional location: SBA lending activity and median black family income.

SBA Loans by SMSA Regional Location

Receipt of SBA loans in the years inclusive of the two year period 1971, 1972 and of the two year period 1976, 1977 were found to be systematically related to regional location with a Chi-Square of 59.3 and 60.4 respectively. These are both significant at better than the .0001 level of significance. Again, this suggests that a regional interaction term is warranted in regard to these two variables (See Tables 2.14 and 2.15).

Descriptively, it is apparent from Table 2.14 that the South over the 1971, 1972 period was disproportionately under represented in the receivership of SBA funds. Virtually, 55 percent of Southern metropolitan areas had under $5 in SBA funds per black capita compared to 8.8 percent of Midwest SMSAs, 10 percent of SMSAs in the West, and 15.4 percent of Northeastern SMSAs. While no SMSA in the South had $30 or more in per capita SBA loans in this period, 20 percent of the SMSAs in the West, 14.7 percent of Midwest SMSAs and 11.5 percent of Northeastern SMSAs were in this category. Moreover, (i) 22 percent of all SMSAs having greater than $15 in SBA funds per capita were located in the West although it contained 13 percent of all the SMSAs, (ii) 29 percent of all the SMSAs of greater than $15 per capita in SBA funds were located in the Northeast, which contained 17 percent of all SMSAs, (iii) 37 percent of all SMSAs in the over $15 per capita category were in the Midwest which contained 22 percent of all SMSAs; and (iv) only 12 percent of all SMSAs in the 15 plus category were in the South though it contained 48 percent of all SMSAs.

31

Though there were some improvements for the South by the 1976, 1977 period such that the South with 48 percent of the total SMSAs had 41 percent of the SMSAs experiencing greater than $5 <u>increases</u> in per capita SBA loans, it still had but 17 percent of the SMSAs experiencing greater than $10 per capita increases in SBA monies. In addition, table 2.17 indicates that while none of the SMSAs in the West had less than $5 per capita in SBA funds during the 1976, 1977 period, the South still had 47 percent of all SMSAs experiencing such low levels. Because of the extremely initial low levels of 1971, 1972 funding in the South, significant increases in SBA funding still left the South with <u>no</u> SMSAs in either of the two highest categories of funding by 1976, 1977 of over $30 and $50 per capita. The West and Midwest while accounting for 35 percent of all SMSAs, accounted for 82 percent of all SMSAs in the greater than $30 per capita categories (See Table 2.16).

TABLE 2-14

DISTRIBUTION OF SBA LOANS IN SMSA's BY REGION, 1971 AND 1972

($ PER BLACK CAPITA)

TABLE 2-14

	Neg. to Zero	0 - 5	5 - 15	15 - 30	30 - 50	50 and Over	SMSA's in Region as % of All SMSA's
Northeast (N = 26)							
Percent of SMSA's in NE Region	7.7	7.7	30.8	42.3	3.8	7.7	16.8
Percent of all SMSA's across all Regions	40.0	4.4	14.3	29.7	14.3	40.0	
North Central (N = 34)							
Percent of SMSA's in NC Region	2.9	5.9	38.2	38.2	8.8	5.9	21.9
Percent of all SMSA's across all Regions	20.0	4.4	23.3	35.1	42.9	40.0	
South (N = 75)							
Percent of SMSA's in South	2.7	52.0	37.3	8.0	0.0	0.0	48.4
Percent of all SMSA's across all Regions	40.0	86.7	50.0	16.2	0.0	0.0	
West (N = 20)							
Percent of SMSA's in West	0.0	10.0	35.0	35.0	15.0	5.0	12.9
Percent of all SMSA's in all Regions	0.0	4.4	12.5	18.9	42.9	20.0	

$X^2 = 59.33$ (15 degrees of freedom)

TABLE 2-15

TABLE 2-15   DISTRIBUTION OF SBA LOANS IN SMSA's BY REGION, 1976 and 1977
($ Per Black Capita)

	Neg. to Zero	0-5	5-15	15-30	30-50	50 and Over	SMSA's in Region % of all SMSA's
Northeast (N = 26)							
Percent of SMSA's in NE Region	7.7	7.7	60.0	26.9	3.8	3.8	
Percent of all SMSA's across all Regions	40.0	5.0	19.1	22.6	12.5	33.3	16.8
North Central (N = 34)							
Percent of SMSA's in NC Region	5.9	11.8	38.2	29.4	8.8	5.9	
Percent of all SMSA's across all Regions	40.0	10.0	19.1	32.3	37.5	66.7	21.9
South (N = 75)							
Percent of SMSA's in South	1.3	45.3	46.7	6.7	0.0	0.0	
Percent of all SMSA's across all Regions	20.0	85.0	51.5	16.1	0.0	0.0	48.4
West (N = 20)							
Percent of SMSA's in West	0.0	0.0	35.0	45.0	20.0	0.0	
Percent of all SMSA's in all Regions	0.0	0.0	10.3	29.0	50.0	0.0	12.9

$X^2 = 60.42$ (15 degrees of freedom)

TABLE 2-16

CHANGE IN SBA LOANS TO SMSA's BY REGION
($ PER BLACK CAPITA)

TABLE 2-16

	Neg. to Zero	0 - 1.5	1.5 - 3.0	3.0 - 5.0	5.0 - 10.0	10.0+	SMSA's in Region as % of all SMSA's
Northeast (N = 26)							
Percent of SMSA's in NE Region	57.7	11.5	3.8	3.8	11.5	11.5	
Percent of all SMSA's across all Regions	18.8	20.0	7.7	12.5	14.3	16.7	16.8
North Central (N = 34)							
Percent of SMSA's in NC Region	52.9	2.9	8.8	5.9	8.8	20.6	
Percent of all SMSA's across all Regions	22.5	6.7	3.1	25.0	14.3	38.9	21.9
South (N = 75)							
Percent of SMSA's in South	46.7	13.3	12.0	6.7	17.3	4.0	
Percent of all SMSA's across all Regions	43.8	66.7	69.2	62.5	61.9	16.7	48.4
West (N = 20)							
Percent of SMSA's in West	60.0	5.0	0.0	0.0	10.0	25.0	
Percent of all SMSA's in all Regions	15.0	6.7	0.0	0.0	9.5	27.8	12.9

$X^2 = 19.78$ (15 degrees of freedom)

Black Median Family Income

The combination of low initial starting position and modest gains in the South and large, significant gains in the West is also reflected in black median income. In 1972, the South had nearly 80 percent of its SMSAs averaging less than $6,000 in Black median family income, whereas the Northeast and Midwest had no SMSAs in those lowest categories; and the West had 20 percent of its SMSAs in those categories (Table 2.17). The Midwest dominated the list of high income SMSAs in 1972, with 54.5 percent of all SMSAs with over $8,500 in black family income being located in that region though it contained but 22 percent of all SMSAs sampled. The South by contrast had 48.4 percent of all SMSAs located in its region, but only 9.1 percent of the SMSAs in the highest category. Table 2.18 indicates that by 1977, improvement in black family income in the South resulted in only 12 percent of the Southern SMSAs having less than $10,000 in black median family income though no other region had an SMSA in this category. Whereas the Midwest had nearly 55 percent of the SMSAs in the highest income category in 1970, it contained but 36 perent of the SMSAs in the highest income category by 1980. By 1980, the Northeast, Midwest and South all had between 29 and 32 percent of their SMSAs experiencing increases in black median family income of under $6,000, whereas the West had only 15 percent of its SMSAs in these lowest categories. Moreover, though the West contained 12.9 percent of all the SMSAs studied, it had 29 percent of those SMSAs which experienced growth in black median family income in excess of $10,000.

To summarize, we have observed that there is fairly wide variation in the patterns of growth of black business ownership by SMSA. Wide ranging variation exists for growth in per capita receipts, total number of firms and formation rates. Consistenly, however, we find smaller variations in failure rates: First, there are no statistically signficiant differences in failure rates among minority racial/ethnic groups. Second, the range of failure rates for black-owned enterprises are less than half of those for formation rates. This suggests that while an analysis of black-owned firm failures is important, a clear understanding of the lower business participation rates of blacks requires a special emphasis on the determinants of entrepreneurial choice at the outset.

TABLE 2-17   MEDIAN BLACK FAMILY INCOME IN SMSA's BY REGION, 1972   Table 2-17

	Less than 4,000	4 - 5,000	5 - 6,000	6 - 7,000	7 - 8500	8500 +	SMSA's in Region as % of all SMSA's
Northeast (N = 26)							
Percent of SMSA's in NE Region	0.0	0.0	0.0	42.3	50.0	7.7	
Percent of all SMSA across all Regions	0.0	0.0	0.0	28.2	31.0	18.2	16.8
North Central (N = 34)							
Percent of SMSA's in NC Region	0.0	0.0	0.0	26.5	55.9	17.6	
Percent of all SMSA's across all Regions	0.0	0.0	0.0	23.1	45.2	54.5	21.9
South (N = 75)							
Percent of SMSA's in South	4.0	41.3	33.3	17.3	2.7	1.3	
Percent of all SMSA's across all Regions	100.0	93.9	92.6	33.3	4.8	9.1	48.4
West (N = 20)							
Percent of SMSA's in West	0.0	10.0	10.0	30.0	40.0	10.0	
Percent of all SMSA's in all Regions	0.0	6.1	7.4	15.4	19.0	18.2	12.9

X^2 = 100.66   (15 degrees of freedom)

TABLE 2-18

TABLE 2-18   MEDIAN BLACK FAMILY INCOME IN SMSA's BY REGION, 1977

	Less than 8,000	8-10,000	10-12,000	12-14,000	14-17,000	17,000+	SMSA's in Region as % of all SMSA's
		($ THOU)					
Northeast (N = 26)							
Percent of SMSA's in NE Region	0.0	0.0	11.5	57.7	19.2	11.5	
Percent of all SMSA's across all Regions	0.0	0.0	8.1	20.8	19.2	27.3	16.8
North Central (N = 34)							
Percent of SMSA's in NC Region	0.0	0.0	0.0	52.9	35.3	11.8	
Percent of all SMSA's across all Regions	0.0	0.0	0.0	25.0	46.2	36.4	21.9
South (N = 75)							
Percent of SMSA's in South	1.3	10.7	41.3	38.7	5.3	2.7	
Percent of all SMSA's across all Regions	100.0	100.0	83.8	40.3	15.4	18.2	48.4
West (N = 20)							
Percent of SMSA's in West	0.0	0.0	15.0	50.0	25.0	10.0	
Percent of all SMSA's in all Regions	0.0	0.0	8.1	13.9	19.2	18.2	12.9

$X^2 = 49.44$ (15 degrees of freedom)

TABLE 2-19

GROWTH IN MEDIAN FAMILY INCOME IN SMSA's BY REGION
(\$ Thou)

TABLE 2-19

	2-4,000	4-6,000	6-8,000	8-10,000	10,000 and Over	SMSA's in Region as a % of All SMSA's
Northeast						
Percent of SMSA's in NE Region	7.7	30.8	42.8	11.5	7.7	16.8
Percent of all SMSA's across all Regions	100.0	17.8	12.9	18.8	28.6	
North Central						
Percent of SMSA's in NC Region	0.0	29.4	55.9	8.8	5.9	21.9
Percent of all SMSA's across all Regions	0.0	22.2	22.4	18.8	28.6	
South						
Percent of SMSA's in South	0.0	32.0	58.7	8.0	1.3	48.4
Percent of all SMSA's across all Regions	0.0	53.3	51.8	37.5	14.3	
West						
Percent of SMSA's in West	0.0	15.0	55.0	20.0	10.0	12.9
Percent of all SMSA's in all Regions	0.0	6.7	12.9	25.0	28.6	

$X^2 = 18.54$ (12 degrees of freedom)

Chapter III

LITERATURE REVIEW

The existing literature on minority business ownership has been principally concerned with explaining the relatively underdeveloped character of the minority business sector. Most studies specific to the black-owned business sector begin with an acknowledgement of the well observed fact that the typical black business is small, is in the retail trade or personal services sector, and that the black business sector as a whole provides relatively little employment and income for the black working population. These studies suggest a variety of explanations for the historical performance of black-owned businesses and why they are marginal relative to the business community as a whole. While there have been some attempts to do empirical tests to verify the importance of some postulated factors, for the most part these explanations have been ad-hoc and speculative. This is most notable for studies conducted in this area up through 1980. In this regard, a widely disseminated 1984 paper by the Minority Business Development Agency on minority-owned business problems and opportunities noted:

> Minority business development has been a federal public policy concern for almost twenty years, but a concerted effort to carefully research the characteristics and problems of those firms began only three years ago. Most studies completed as of 1980 were based more on the researcher's opinion, rather than accepted methodology and appropriate data. Consequently, public officials were too often guided by stereotype images of the minority-owned business.[1]

In general, research conducted before 1981 did not include any direct analysis of the determinants of the overall performance of the black-owned business sector, nor of formation and failure rates by either industry or geographical location. Nonetheless, the factors identified in this literature as explanations for the relatively underdeveloped nature of black business firms are suggestive of factors that should influence the rate of formations and failures in the black- owned business sector. One purpose of this literature review is to extract these factors. Although this earlier literature lacks a consistent conceptual framework, we have identified four factors which have been consistently put forward in this literature as possible explanations for the limited development of black business ownership: limited market demand, limited capital resources, limited know-how and efficiency (human capital; small scale), and racial exclusion (discrimination). Although various authors have placed heavier emphasis on different factors, most of the arguments incorporate more than one factor. Frequently, all of the causes are seen as interdependent.

While the research conducted after 1980 differs from previous work regarding both the nature of issues addressed and the techniques used to explore these issues, we have, by and large, integrated these later works in a way that is consistent with the four factor framework mentioned above. This most recent body of work is largely summarized in the sections on equity capital and debt structure, role models and the social status of business ownership, industry trends of minority-owned firms, and models of business growth.

LIMITED DEMAND

The limited market size argument appears in the literature many times. General impacts of the lack of access to markets, due to various reasons, have been outlined in Bates and Bradford,[2] Brimmer,[3] Markwalder,[4] Wallich,[5] and Brimmer and Terrell.[6] In essence, this argument suggests that the black owned business sector has little growth potential because it is restricted to serving the black community. This restriction is seen as a result of segregation, discrimination and choice. In any case, it is argued that given the limited demand which results from the relatively limited incomes, high rates of unemployment, poverty, and cyclical instability characteristic of the black community, the development potential of black businesses is limited.

Brimmer and Terrell suggest that the austere market conditions caused by the low income and high unemployment in black communities severely restrict both the size of black businesses and opportunities for expansion. They maintain that because of the limited markets provided by the black community the opportunity cost of investing resources and personnel in black businesses is too high when compared to outside investment possibilities. Brimmer and Terrell further argue that the limited market open to black enterpreneurs does not provide profitable enough opportunities for the best black talent to choose entrepreneurship over wage and salary employment. In their view this generates a rational response in the form of fewer choices for a self-employed business career by educated and professional blacks.

A link between business efficiency and the extent of the market was also proposed by Wallich in discussing whether black businessmen should limit themselves to segregated markets or pursue business opportunities wherever they exist. He found that black businessmen cannot count on white patronage, and as a result of the limit this places on their sales growth they find it more difficult to raise capital than their white counterparts. Moreover, according to Wallich, because of limited markets, black businesses have a difficult time reaching a level of operations that would bring their costs down to competitive levels.

Brimmer argued that much of the success that blacks have enjoyed in areas such as restaurants, hotels, insurance companies, and banks was possible because of the protection provided by segregation. These markets were in a sense reserved for black entrepreneurs. However, as legal restraints against racial discrimination are removed, and as black family income increases, he predicts that these markets may be lost to larger more efficient white owned businesses. Ong[7] tested the hypothesis that demand for black business output decreases as desegregation increases, and black per capita income increases. However, he found no evidence of statistical significance to support this hypothesis.

The sensitivity of black businesses to overall economic conditions has been discussed by Bradford and Bates, Brimmer, Markwalder, and Brimmer and Terrell, among others. The upshot of these discussions is that traditional black businesses are disproportionately impacted by economic downturns. This follows since traditional businesses sell more heavily to lower income ghetto clientele, who during downturns in the economy are more adversely affected than other consumers. Thus, during such downturns, their low-income customers lower their purchases from local restaurants, beauty parlors, laundry mats, and other local retail establishments to a greater extent than do the customers of other businesses. Bradford and Bates, however, argue that the disproportionate sensitivity of traditional black businesses to the business cycle does not hold for emerging black businesses in manufacturing, construction, and wholesale trade.

This literature, taken as a whole, strongly suggests that the propensity of black businesses to serve an almost exclusively black clientele is a major cause of the relatively low level of participation in black business ownership. However, little concrete evidence is offered to support this speculation. In fact, the evidence offered to support this conjecture could be used to support the opposite conclusion, namely the focus on serving the needs of the black community is the major factor which facilitated the little business development we do observe. Moreover, the size of the black consumer market is many times larger than the size of the black business sector. This fact suggests that the size of the market in the black community by itself may not be the primary constraint to black business development. Black businesses have been unable to capture anything near a major share of the black consumer dollar and have had considerably less success capturing the non-black consumer dollar. This apparently results from other factors which limit the ability of black businesses to effectively compete for available markets.

This literature suggests, on the one hand, that a high degree of segregation in markets for business output should be a positive factor in the level of black business ownership. However, the literature is not consistent on the impact of desegregation on black business development. On the one hand, authors like Brimmer and Terrell, and Ong suggest that desegregation should hurt black businesses by removing a protective barrier against competition. On the other hand, other authors like Bates seem to imply that desegregation should help nontraditional, emerging lines of operation by opening up access to broader markets. The literature also seems to suggest that growth in the available black consumer market should be an important determinant of the rate of growth of black business ownership. However, there is also the argument that increased affluence will cause black consumers to seek purchases in the white sector and might also induce more competition from the white business sector. The most recent study by Handy and Swinton[8] found that greater levels of market demand were a significant influence on both total firm growth and receipt growth of black-owned firms, while residential segregation was of little or no importance. In short, the predictions of this literature are ambiguous.

LIMITED ACCESS TO FINANCIAL CAPITAL

Overall Analyses

Another factor that has been traditionally recognized as a barrier to black business ownership is a general limited access to capital. General discussions of the impact of limited access to capital markets have been presented by Bates and Bradford,[9] Bates,[10] Dominquez,[11] Osborne and Granfield,[12] Hunter and Sinkley[13] and Ong,[14] among others. Bates, identified this as the major reason that black businesses have generally been of limited size. The lack of capital has been repeatedly identified in surveys as a major reason for the limited development of the black owned business sector (Young and Hund).[15] For authors who emphasize the lack of available capital this factor plays a more significant role than limited market size. In fact, the literature as a whole suggests that the propensity of black businesses to serve a limited, mainly black clientele is most directly linked to the limited availability of capital.

The basic arguments are discussed most notably in Bates, Bradford and Bates, and Osborne and Granfield. These studies suggest the view that black businesses have been concentrated in the traditional industries, (restaurants, laundries, barber shops, and other predominantly small service and retail establishments serving the black community) because these small scale businesses consistently require

46

significantly less capital than businesses in construction, manufacturing and wholesale trade. Black businesses which have been found in the non-traditional areas, it is concluded, generally have been under capitalized relative to their real capital needs. The restricted access to capital has limited black entrepreneurs to operating small scale enterprises in less promising product lines.

Researchers have found, moreover, that the level of capitalization is significantly correlated with the business success of individual black firms. Osborne and Granfield point out that after controlling for product line, non-failing emerging black firms had a capitalization of $171,000 which was $50,000 more than the average emerging black firm and $90,000 more than emerging black firms which failed. Bates and Bradford show the emerging black firms' profits would increase by 24¢ for every dollar increase in net investment. These writers also conclude that because of their limited access to capital, blacks have historically had to concentrate in circumscribed, traditional fields precisely because they can be started and maintained with little capital. The inference to be drawn is that the skewed distribution of types of businesses in black communities and their limited size and rate of growth are the result of the limited availability of outside capital and limited retained earnings of small ghetto enterprises.

In an analysis which compares SBA financed firms to firms in a National Business League Survey, Bates finds that if adequately capitalized, emerging black businesses in the areas of transportation, construction, manufacturing and wholesaling offer an economic potential far greater than implied by the Brimmer and Terrell assessment. Bates concluded that increasing the supply of capital to the black business community can be socially productive. In his view the main bottleneck to black business development has been the limited amounts of capital market access available to black firms in non-traditional areas.

Equity Capital and Debt Structure

During the initial stages of a firm's development, the entrepreneur-owner must inevitably raise private funds either from their own personal wealth or from family and friends. Research in this area concerning minority business enterprises is virtually nonexistent. The importance of equity capital in general, however, was largely confirmed by Bearse[16] who found that family financial assets were strongly, positively correlated with the likelihood of individuals becoming entrepreneurs. Such assets were lowest among blacks, with Hispanics and Asian-Americans highest. In fact, Asians had family assets which were comparable to white businessmen in the noncorporate sector. This may largely explain the relatively high formation rates among Asians compared to blacks.

The impact of raising capital funds through borrowing from financial intermediaries has been investigated, in part, by Bates, Furino, and Wadsworth.[17] They found that minority-owned firms had higher debt-equity ratios than similarly sized non-minority firms. They found that firms which failed had less liquidity than those that survived since high debt to equity ratios caused liquidity problems in their ability to pay current bills. Moreover, this problem occurred across all lines of operation including the traditional areas of retail sales and personal services, as well as in the emerging lines of manufacturing and business services. This liquidity problem is the result of minority-owned firms beginning operations with inadequate equity capital, and taking on excessive amounts of debt financing. Furthermore, Bates, Furino, and Wadsworth found that minority firm debt is principally long term, and that they are not taking advantage of short-term trade credit. Liquidity problems, they found, however, tend to decrease as the firm matures and becomes older.

Small Business Administration Assistance

Another body of the literature relevant to understanding the importance of the capital constraint focuses on studying the impact and role of the Small Business Administration. The impact of the Small Business Administration in filling the void of capital funds to black businesses has been discussed in Doctors and Lockwood,[18] Bates,[19] Bates and Bradford,[20] Doctors and Wokutch[21] and Yancy.[22] The discussion of the importance of capital might lead one to expect that the provision of loan capital by the SBA could lead to higher rates of growth of minority businesses. Most of the literature on the SBA, however, focuses on studying the patterns of SBA lending and the performance of assisted firms. There were no studies that analyzed the impact of SBA loan programs on the overall rate of growth of black businesses.

The earliest research in this area examined the loan repayment performance of assisted businesses and concluded that the debt retirement record of black client firms was poor. Doctors and Lockwood found that a higher percentage of SBA liquidations and disposals, and charge-offs occurred in black business having zero employees. While 24 percent of randomly selected minority firms had zero employees, 43 percent of the charge-off business failures receiving SBA money had zero employees. Overall, between 1968 and 1971, black businesses accounted for 82 percent of the charge-offs and 85 percent of the liquidations and disposals of minority businesses, while accounting for 64 percent of the total loans made to minority businesses. In 1971 alone, black businesses comprised 22.4 percent of all SBA loans but accounted for 50 percent of all charge-off and liquidations. Bates similarly found that almost 50 percent of the black firms that had received SBA guaranteed loans in New York and Boston were delinquent in their loan payments with 34 percent of them in liquidation. These findings indicated to Doctors and Lockwood that smaller black enterprises are riskier than larger black enterprises, and that SBA policy should be more directed at aiding larger-scaled black business enterprises.

According to Bates and Bradford, while SBA established the Economic Opportunity Loan (EOL) Program in 1964 to help impoverished businessmen, this program was not designed to foster the success and development of the overall minority-owned business community. Seventy percent of all loans to minorities came from EOL funds, but such loans were found to be greatly inferior to other SBA loan programs in its overall impact on the success of minority businesses. First, because EOL default rates were found to be significantly higher than 7A and 8A loans to minority businesses. Second, because the EOL program actually perpetuated rather than alleviated poverty among low-income, disadvantaged entrepreneurs since borrowers had to continue to meet SBA loan payments after delinquency and liquidation.

Investigating 106 black firms in Atlanta from 1969 to 1971, Yancy concluded that, first, there were no significant differences between SBA assisted black businesses and unassisted black businesses in terms of profitability, employment, and organizational form; and, second, that the number of black firms created through SBA lending policy tends to be offset by failures and discontinuances. He concluded overall that federal programs like SBA have had no measurable impact on the status of black business, and that improvements in black businesses are positively correlated with improvements in the overall economic condition of the black community.

The SBA literature as a whole would tend to suggest that SBA lending programs are not effective in generating successful firms in the black business sector. The primary reason for this is related to poor client selection and the relatively modest size of the SBA program. None of the studies mentioned thus far, however, performed any direct analysis on the impact of SBA loans on the growth of the black business sector in the various SMSAs. Handy and Swinton, however, on performing such a test found that SBA was a significant factor in total black firm growth and receipt growth outside the South. This last study however made no attempt to investigate the impact of SBA loans on formation and failure rates of the black-owned business sector across SMSAs nor across industries.

Black Commercial Banking

One final set of studies that are relevant to the capital availability factor is those studies which have explored the role of black banks in financing minority business enterprises. The ability of black commercial banks to finance the business development in communities they serve has been analyzed by Bates and Bradford,[23] Andrew Brimmer,[24] Ed Irons,[25] and John Boorman.[26] The major issue is whether or not the existence of black banks generally imply greater access to capital for black owned businesses.

Bates and Bradford found that black banks have expanded in a steady two-dimensional growth pattern since 1960, whereby (i) existing institutions have grown steadily in terms of deposits and asset holdings, and (ii) the number of banks in existence has more than quadrupled. In 1974, 41 black-owned banks were operating in the United States with 31 of these having been formed during the twelve years of 1962 to 1974. The mere existence of black-owned banks, however, as Bates and Bradford point out, does not guarantee that they will serve as vehicles for financing economic development of their communities.

Andrew Brimmer, former member of the Federal Reserve Board of Governors, has in fact argued that black banks as a group appear to possess very little potential as instruments of urban economic development. Black banks in his opinion are poorly managed and suffer from high operating costs and loan losses. They are handicapped by (a) a severe shortage of management talent and (b) a local market environment too risky for small banks to lend money. Moreover, Brimmer finds that black banks channel a significant share of their deposits into U.S. government securities, thereby, possibly diverting resources from the black community into financing the national debt.

Both Brimmer and Irons, a former director of the National Bankers Association, concluded that,

(i) Lack of experienced management and banking expertise caused inefficient operations.

(ii) High costs were related to both poor management and the fact that black banks attract a large number of small, highly active deposit accounts.

(iii) Large loan losses stemming from the characteristics of the ghetto market led to eroding profits.

Irons, however, in a criticism of Brimmer's work, points out that newer black banks behave and perform differently than the older ones. When Irons compared black banks with white banks in the same cities and same age categories, he found that black banks faired favorably with white banks in terms of income, but unfavorably in terms of expenses.

Both Brimmer and Irons concur that the black business structure must become more diverse and profitable for black banks to become viable. Only then can the black commercial infra-structure provide both the deposit activity and base for sound loans required to make black banking significant in their communities.

John Boorman, an economist with the Federal Deposit Insurance Corporation, confirms to an even greater extent Irons' assertion that trends in minority banking show improvement. In one of the most comprehensive series of studies of minority commercial banking to date, Boorman found that improvement in performance of black banks were quite pronounced as they became more mature. Boorman used time series data from 1964 to 1972, whereas Brimmer and Irons looked only at black banking performance cross sectionally for one year. By using this better measure, Boorman was able to show that the operating efficiency of black banks relative to majority banks compares unfavorably during the initial years of operation but quite favorably, thereafter; and that their ability to generate gross income per dollar of assets is almost identical. The ratio of operating income to total assets for minority banks on the average rose from 2.72 percent in 1964 to 6.04 percent by 1972, whereas nonminority banks showed an increase from 3.14 to 5.93 percent over the same time period. Measuring inefficiency by the ratio of operating expenses to total assets, Boorman found that while this inefficiency ratio increased from 4.35 percent in 1964 to 5.74 percent in 1972 for minority banks, nonminority banks inefficiency ratio increased from 3.52 to 5.20 over this same period. Consequently, minority banks do show greater difficulty in generating profits in their early years of operation, but they improve considerably over time. The problem of relative profit positions of minority banks according to Boorman stems not from the ratio of gross income to assets, which is typically as high as for majority banks, but in its variability which is also much higher. However, this appears to occur, again, primarily because operating expenses are particularly high for minority banks during the first five years.

Bates and Bradford support the position that newer black banks once they reach maturity (i.e., after five years) are probably better able to finance business development. They cite the fact that newer black banks are more active participants in FHA-HUD and VA mortgage programs, and also in SBA loan insurance programs than are older banks founded in the 1920s and 1930s. The protection against default risk offered by these programs enables newer banks to protect themselves at least partially against higher risks in their loan demand function. Bates and Bradford, thereby, expect this fact coupled with older banks' reported lower loan loss reserves to mean that newer black banks would be more likely to service loan demands of black households and businesses. They further point out, however, that it is not clearly understood to what degree black banks actually serve as vehicles for financing economic development in their communities. If black banks are conservative, highly risk averse institutions that prefer government bonds and bills to holdings of business and household loans and mortgages, then they may not be helping to finance economic development in communities they serve. Bates and Bradford note, however, that despite government regulations constraining the way government deposits may be invested, loans as a percentage of assets have clearly risen as the number of newer banks have increased since 1970.

This literature, therefore, suggests that black banks may be a factor in increasing the rate of growth of the black business sector. However, the literature as a whole seem to suggest that black banks should not be expected to be a major factor because of their small size and relatively conservative banking practices.

LIMITED BUSINESS HUMAN CAPITAL

Several authors have focused on the lack of business human capital (formal training, experience, management skills) as the dominant explanation for the limited development of the black owned business sector. According to these authors, limited business human capital leads black businesses to low efficiency and low profits.This in turn reduces their ability to compete for proportionate market shares and for financial capital. The paucity of managerial skills, business knowledge and experience has been emphasized by Foley,[27] Coles,[28] Strang,[29] Brimmer[30] and Case.[31] This, therefore, becomes another explanation for the limited level of development of the black business sector.

According to Foley, the primary reason for low credit ratings of black businesses is the inadequate management ability of black business borrowers. Racial factors in Foley's view are clearly less important than commercial banks' assessment of the borrower's management ability. Strang similarly concludes, after assessing survey information on 100 black firms that the high incidence of failures of black businesses is attributable to a lack of managerial ability, business education and experience. Like Foley, Strang claimed that black enterprises had incompetent management of budgets, and poor marketing and sales programs. Though Brimmer emphasizes lack of markets as an explanation for the low rates of growth of black businesses, he too suggests that black enterpreneurs are not sufficiently prepared for the managerial and technical requisites of new fields or large scale enterprises to be competitive in newer expanding markets. Flournoy Coles found that of the 564 black enterprises he surveyed in seven urban areas in

1969, not one of the owners or managers had formal business training. Coles emphasizes that deficient management, marketing and technical abilities are reflected in the fact that too many black businesses are concentrated in high risk enterprises in limited markets. However, none of these authors compared black entrepreneurs to a control group of white entrepreneurs.

In contrast, a study which included a central group of white firms (Scott, Furino, and Rodriquez),[32] concluded that poor performance of minority owned firms is due less to personal skill differences of minorities than to structural factors of smaller size, younger age, and poorer industry location as dictated by the available market. According to these researchers, knowing whether a firm is minority-owned does not predict performance independent of structural factors. They find specifically that once asset size and age are controlled for, the mean rate of return on assets is no lower for minority than for majority firms, nor is the failure rate any higher. One limitation of their study, however, is that the Dun and Bradstreet data files used in their study tend to overrepresent the more mature creditworthy firms. From an econometric standpoint, of course, this is not too serious a problem since the same level of credit-worthiness is possessed by the control group of majority-owned firms. Moreover, by controlling for structural factors, and comparing both minority and majority small business of similar size, this analysis more accurately reflects the relative performance of minority entrepreneurs independent of limited opportunities. A critical issue, however, is whether structural factors like size of firm and poor industry designation are, in fact, exogenous factors. Brimmer for instance has argued that such factors are in essence endogenous since limited business capital, personal skills and purposeful pursuit of limited markets can themselves be causes of the skewed structural characteristics of minority firms.

In any case, these studies do suggest that the performance of black owned businesses should be related to the level of human capital possessed by black entrepreneurs. This, therefore, suggests another factor that should be incorporated into our analysis.

ROLE MODELS AND SOCIAL STATUS OF BUSINESS OWNERSHIP

Chen and Stevens[33] have interpreted some of the findings of Bates[34] and Handy and Swinton[35] as indicating an improved influence of positive role models in the minority community. They cite evidence that suggests that over fifty percent of all entrepreneurs have parents or close relatives who own businesses. However, definitive statistics are not available to support or refute this hypothesis in the minority business community. Chen and Stevens interpret Bates' finding of a shift in the average profile of the minority entrepreneur toward younger, higher income entrepreneurs in emerging lines of operations as reflecting an improved social status in business ownership among minority youth. Handy and Swinton found that both higher initital levels of black professionals and managers in the black community and increases in those levels over time were significant positive factors in explaining total receipt growth in black-owned businesses and growth in black-owned firms with paid employees. Chen and Stevens viewed this finding as indirectly picking up influences of positive role models as well as improvements in business knowledge.

Chen and Stevens claim that the entrepreneurial role models available to minorities in 1960 were few in number and may have exerted a negative attitude toward business ownership as an occupational choice. Minority entrepreneurs through the 1960s earned less income than if they had been employed in a wage or salary position. So aspiring minority youth made the rational decision that they could do better by not becoming entrepreneurs. Their perception of an entreprenuer was someone who worked long hours in a low income and degrading line of business such as personal services. But during the 1970s, according to Chen and Stevens, this profile of minority entrepreneurs began to improve, with a small group of younger and better educated entrepreneurs in emerging non-traditional lines of business. Nonetheless, Bates found that in 1980, most young well-educated minorities were choosing the professions or management, rather than self-employment as career occupations. This is particularly true among blacks, and may be an important reason why black business formation rates are lower than other groups. Minority entrepreneurship, however, is showing definite signs of improvement.

RACIAL DISCRIMINATION

Authors who emphasize discrimination as a primary factor of black business performance argue that racial discrimination limits access to markets, limits access to financial capital, limits access to business knowledge and contracts, limits access to credit and risk capital, and in general, impedes the full participation of black business owners in American commerce. These limits, in turn reduce the ability of black firms to operate efficienctly and/or earn a normal profit. It forces black firms to remain small and operate in a limited segment of the market.

Racial discrimination has been highlighted as primary cause of low minority business growth rates, low formation rates, and high business failures by Cross,[36] Lee,[37] Glover,[38] Lowery and Associates,[39] and Jackson and King.[40] The importance of racial discrimination in limiting market and resource access has been argued most forcefully by Cross in a little known paper on black capitalism.

Cross asserts that the purposeful withholding of economic demand for the goods and services of black producers by the predominant white society has in itself caused (1) black capital to shrink, (2) black male labor force participation to diminish, (3) black people to tire of arming themselves with skills, and (4) black manufacturers to suspend or lose interest in production. For Cross, the shortage of black bankers, accountants, engineers, lawyers, and managers is simply a fulfillment of the prediction of classical economics--the direct result of sustained withdrawal of serious economic demand for black people in these larger economic roles. Moreover, the discrimination of whites against blacks has, according to Cross, predictably curtailed the supply of entrepreneurs and producers because the economy never furnished adequate wants or demands for goods that might be made, sold or serviced by black people.

> If conventional wisdom about black people missing a tradition of entrepreneurship, ownership, and "need for achievement" holds even a grain of truth, it is a statement--not of an original condition--but of an assured economic result of the solid and sustained preference of white people not to trade or exchange commercial promises with black people... I find it strange that this (increasing the visible supply of black people who are trained entrepreneurs and professionals) should be the total strategy in a <u>market</u> economy where the best way to increase the supply of something you want has always been to make sure there was a very solid demand for it. 41

Lee in a thorough discussion of the history of black business gives voluminous evidence to support the contention that black businesses and black professionals have always been successful in markets either left to them or in markets where they have been freely allowed to compete. Hunter and Sinkleycontend that minority owned businesses have been socially constrained from access to conventional capital markets and have, therefore, significantly higher levels of failure probability than majority firms. Cross also maintains that black businesses are, in effect, isolated by a system of tariffs on retail sales, rents, and consumer and business credit, and are consequently viewed as not worthy of credit and risk captial.

The problem of discrimination faced by blacks attempting to sell such products and services to the larger white community has been emphasized by Glover, and Lowery and Associates. Market entry is seen as a special problem for blacks trying to move into non-traditional, emerging businesses as recommended by Bates and others. In their Procurement and Marketing Handbook, the Minority Contractors Assistance Project states..."not one white contractor, we interviewed believed that a minority contractor could offer a competitive bid..." Glover submits it is difficult for minority contractors to market their services for jobs which have been considered "white jobs."

As in much of the rest of the literature, rigorous empirical test of these hypotheses are generally missing. Case studies and anecdotal evidence is the rule. Nonetheless, this literature does suggest that black business sectors ought to perform better in SMSA's generally characterized by less discrimination.

INDUSTRY TRENDS OF MINORITY BUSINESS ENTERPRISES

Any analysis of the industry composition of minority business enterprises inevitably must begin with the widely known fact that minority businesses are concentrated in retail sales and personal services. Almost 70 percent of all minority firms are either in retail or personal services. The conventional argument (Brimmer and Terrell,[42] Brimmer,[43] Coles,[44] Foley,[45] Jackson and King[46]) is that in the past segregated, minority-oriented retail and personal service markets provided no significant barriers to entry for minority entrepreneurs. These authors argue that since these markets were at the time virtually ignored by larger, more efficient majority firms, minority firms addressing themselves specifically to their own communities did not need to compete with majority firms concerning optimal capital requirements, cost and economices of scales, product quality and product differentiation, advertising, and marketing and distribution strategies.

With the advent of desegregation, which to a greater degree pitted all businesses in the same product line against one another, some reserachers concluded that smaller, more inefficient minority entreprises would fall by the wayside. Black business enterprises, in particular, were viewed as small and inefficient; and located in slow growing retail and service industries. Strang[47] reported that black sales increases between 1969-1972 were most notable in transportation, public utilities, wholesale trade, manufacturing, and construction, and slowest in retail and selected services. He concluded, however, that industry mix was not as serious a problem as business size -- with the retail and personal services sector being disproportionately small firms with no paid employees. In this same vein Ando and Sickles[48] found size to be a significant predictor of the probability of failure. Stevens[49] found that the 1972-1977 annual failure rate for all minority firms declined somewhat with larger firm size. Firms in six size intervals ranging from 0 to 99 employees had annual failure rates of 12.0 to 12.9 percent. This was reduced to 9.4 percent for those firms with 100 or more employees. This finding adds support to Birch's earlier conclusion that firms with over 100 employees are better able to survive low points in their pulsations of growth and decline.[50]

Bates in a number of reports[51] has pushed the idea that beneath the aggregate statistics there are two distinct groups within the minority business sector. The first is in traditional lines of business such as personal services and retail trade. He cites the fact that owners in these lines continue to have low education and earnings levels and that these firms show signs of continuous decline. He further claims, however, that entrepreneurs in new lines of emerging business in which minorities have not historically participated are younger, better educated, and tend to have higher earnings. These lines of operation include general contractors, wholesalers, and business and professional services.

Financial characteristics of this group were studied by Bates and Furino [52] using Dun and Bradstreet data on a sample of 5,000 minority-owned firms. With the exception of retail trade, they found that firms in emerging lines of operation were just as profitable as non-minority noncorporate firms. Bates also found a noticeable shift in minority business compostion between 1960 and 1980,: Whereas personal services and retail trade accounted for 54.3% of the minority business sector in 1960, they occupied as a group 35.3% of all minority-owned business in 1980. These are the traditional lines of operation which he has described as having little potential for growth or economic impact. The more emerging lines of operation in transportation, business services, wholesale trade, and finance insurance and real estate nearly doubled as a percent of all minority business from 9.7 to 19 percent between 1960 and 1980.

BUSINESS GROWTH

Studies by Ando and Sickles,[53] and Handy and Swinton[54] investigated the growth of minority-owned firms and black-owned firms respectively. Ando and Sickles found that the minority firms in their sample grew faster than similar non-minority firms. This unexpected finding can be largely attributed to the data set used in their study. They drew firms strictly from the Minority Business Development Agency's assisted firm file. This file was found by Birch, MacCraken and Trainer[55] to be largely composed of high performance, better credit-worthy minority firms. As such Chen and Stevens[56] conclude that the Ando and Sickles study is limited in its usefulness since it employs what they consider to be a highly biased firm file.

Handy and Swinton limited their study to investigating the overall growth of the black-owned business sector in terms of total receipt growth and growth of total number of firms. It did not contain any industry analysis nor any decompostion by firm formation, continuation and failure.

Their analysis conducted over 155 SMSA's containing 100 or more black firms suggests that market demand and resource availability are the two most important general factors influencing the rate of growth of black owned businesses. Greater levels of market demand were a significant influence on both growth in numbers of firms and growth in receipts although the demand factors involved differed somewhat for the two measures of growth. For receipts, the state of the business cycle and the overall level of black consumer purchasing power appeared to be the most significant demand factors. On the other hand, the growth of the local economy and the growth of the black consumer market appeared to be more important factors for firm growth. Moreover, the differential regional impacts for the initial level of black family income suggested that general economic decline in black consumer markets in the SMSAs of the North Central and Northeast had a significantly negative impact on the growth rate of black businesses.

The availability of financial capital also appeared to be a significant factor. For receipt growth, the level of financial capital provided by both SBA and black banks appeared to be a strongly significant factor. The change in SBA capital also was a positive factor in increasing receipt growth. However, the initial levels of SBA activity were not significant in the firm growth equations. This may well be because of the impact of the declining regions. On the other hand, the change in SBA activity was a positive factor in the non-South. There were significant shifts in SBA funding between 1972 and 1977 in the non-South. These shifts appear to have had a benefcial impact on growth in the total number of black-owned firms, but not for firms with paid employees outside of the Western region of the country.

The level and change in the availability of professional and managerial manpower was a surprisingly important factor in the three basic equations. This variable is measured by the number of black individuals employed in professional and managerial occupations in firms which report to the EEOC. Thus, this variable may also be a proxy for the degree of discrimination as well as high level manpower availability. The power of this variable may therefore be at least partially explained by the fact that it also captures variations in the level of discrimination within the SMSA.

While resource availability and market demand appeared to be significant factors, their results provide no confirmation of the importance of segregation, at least as measured by the degree of residential segregation. The existing range of variation in segregation apparently was unrelated to variations in the rate of growth of black-owned businesses. The importance of size was partially confirmed since firm scale was positively associated with growth of firms with paid employees.

LIMITATIONS OF PREVIOUS WORK AND CONTRASTS WITH PRESENT STUDY

Our discussion of the various papers comprising the literature has emphasized their conclusions and their respective areas of coverage of minority business problems. We now turn to a brief discussion of some of the limitations of the literature and how the previous work differs from the present study.

A review of the literature suggests that, on the whole, previous studies are circumscribed by some combination of five limitations. These limitations include, (1) overdependence on voluntary, self-reported questionnaire data from small, poorly selected samples; , (2) nonrecognition of response and selection bias in the type and number of firms analyzed; (3) restriction to single point in time data; (4) the exclusive use of internal factors of the firm with no allowance for larger economic forces; and (5) little or no explicit theoretical framework from which to investigate factors of change and development in minority business enterprise.

Many of these problems can be traced to the paucity of adequate data concerning minority business enterprise since serious, concerted data gathering efforts in this area have been undertaken in only the last ten years or so. The shortcomings of the studies by Brimmer and Terrell, and Coles, for instance, reflect this in large part. Both of these studies, which for several years were considered two of the seminal works in this area, used the 1969 National Business League survey of 564 black business in seven cities. The pattern of data collection in this survey was poor with, for example, only 50 of the 112 business owners responding in Jackson, Mississippi, and 18 of 80 in Durham, North Carolina. Similar response patterns held in the other five cities. Coles, in utilizing only information from a limited number of respondents, leaves his results open to possible significant response bias. Brimmer and Terrell employ a methodology which is seriously hampered by a very questionable assumption that all nonrespondents had zero sales and zero profits. As such, it has extreme built in selectivity bias. In some cases, they report firms with zero sales and positive profits. Moreover, when they regress profits per worker on total receipts, age of owner, and membership in professional or business organization, only 9 percent of the variance in profits is explained. Bates recalculated this same regression using only reported, complete information and found no significant results, with only 2 percent of the variance in profits per worker being explained.

Cases' study consists of a series of discussions and interviews with local black entrepreneurs in Los Angeles. He assembles and interprets their opinions and impressions on minority business problems. Though useful, it certainly cannot be classified as rigorous empirical research.

Yancy's work which seeks to assess the overall impact of federal assistance programs on black business development looks at only one city, Atlanta, using a field study questionnaire covering a 3 month period in 1972. As in the case of the National Business League survey the response rate was very low such that nearly 70 percent of the firms contacted did not respond (i.e., 230 out of 336 firms). Again, response bias is highly probable here too.

Strang's work investigates a small sample of 100 firms from across the country that were in some way assisted by various private and public organizations. These firms appear to be ones that were especially weak in management skills and marketing techniques. The sample is consequently skewed toward the poorly prepared firms. This sample cannot be considered as representing a true cross-section of black businesses nationwide. In general, then, the earlier works in the area relied on survey responses from very limited samples of firms characterized by low response rates and biased sample selection.

Bate's work was the first study which did not rely on data derived strickly from voluntary responses to survey questions by a small number of firms. His research focused on SBA assisted firms and utilized verifiable balance sheet information on assets, liabilities, net worth and liquidity. Though this constituted a distinct improvement in methodology and data, this too was not representative of a cross-section of all black firms. The same criticism can also be leveled at Bates and Bradford which, nontheless, represents a significant improvement over previous work on minority business development and financing.

Though Osborne and Granfield possess a degree of econometric sophistication often lacking in many of the earlier papers in the area, their overall methodological approach has limited generalizability. They investigate the profitability of only 45 black-owned businesses which were assisted by a single California MESBIC. Moreover, they define firm viability as earned profits in one year in excess of MESBIC subsidy capital the preceding year. As Bates correctly points, out a firm earning as much as a a 40 percent rate of return on subsidy capital, which by all normal standards would be deemed as quite successful, does not qualify as viable under their definition. Also, as is true with virtually all the studies in the field, no macro economic factors are considered.

An additional micro-oriented study, discussed previously, which is quite noteworthy is the work of Scott, Furino, and Rodriquez. This study has the advantage of controlling for firm size by comparing minority and majority-owned businesses of the same asset size. Though this answers a certain set of questions

67

regarding the relative profitability and position of firms once size is controlled for, the study is subject to selectivity bias since it only looks at MBDA assisted firms. These firms are on the average more successful and more credit-worthy than minority firms in general. Thus, this selection of firms is skewed toward the very best of minority businesses. It is interesting, and probably quite predictable, that their general assessment of minority business enterprises and the skills of minority entrepreneurs is quite different than that of Strang and Case, and others, whose selection of firms is skewed toward inferior firms.

The studies commissioned by the Minority Business Development Agency in 1983[57] are considered by many in the field to represent the state-of-the-art in minority business research. Many of them, however, can be subjected to much of the same criticism regarding selectivity bias. The Ando and Sickles study, had limited results which could not summarize much concerning minority business failures over time since their observations were limited to a single point in time, and since their sample consisted of the creme-de-la-creme of minority-owned businesses. Birch's study largely confirmed that the results obtained by Furino and Rodriquez, Bates, and Bates, Furino and Wadsworth showing highly successful, profitable minority-owned enterprises, which often exceed the performance of nonminority firms, are a property of the Dun and Bradstreet- MBDA Financial Data Base file used in these studies. We perhaps should not overstate the case however. These studies are excellent, competent works which give many insightful, useful findings. Nonetheless, their results must be understood as a profile of superior-run and managed minority business firms.

The study by Handy and Swinton investigated larger, macro conerns which had simply not been addressed as thoroughly previously. Even here, however, a cautionary flag must be raised. First, no industry analysis was done at all. Second, change in total receipts over the 1972-1977 period, as well as change in total firms, gloss over a number of important issues: Are these substantially the same firms or different firms? What percentage of 1972 firms were still present in 1977? It is critical, in other words, to decompose their results into firms that failed as a group, and firms that succeeded or continued as a group. Also, no analysis was conducted concerning the critical issue of the determinants of business formations. This is important because, as we have previously observed, differences in business participation among different ethic groups are largely a result of significant differences in formation rates and not of differences in failure rates.

The Bearse study used standard demographic variables such as income, education, sex, marital status, and number of children, as well as assets and previous occupation to draw inferences concerning the determinants of entrepreneurial choice. Though useful, there are few extensions and generalizations as what this approach implies concerning the likelihood of entrepreneurial success or failure, or its impact on actual minority business development.

Two other papers which take a macro perspective are Ong and Markwalder. Marwalder's paper is simply a literal descriptive analysis of receipts and number of firms with no specification of causal relationships. His discussion has been criticized elsewhere for drawing conclusions from a broad aggregation which assumes that all service and retail sector firms are similar when, in fact, they are clearly not. Janitorial and housework services are not in the same category as accounting, legal and medical services for instance. Ong's study is the only study outside of Handy and Swinton which specified a causal model using macro factors.

69

It was a useful first step which sought to separate demand and supply factors as a function of a few population and income measures. It did not, however, include any government financial assistance programs, bank loan statistics, professional or managerial data, education levels, experience or unemployment data. Thus, his supply and demand equations are somewhat less than convincing and covers only 30 SMSAs.

This present study, in contrast to the existing literature, will incorporate as explanatory variables SMSA-specific macro factors concerning local state-of-nature risk and opportunity cost conditions, capital access variables, market demand conditions, and business human capital. It will incorporate this framework onto a complete count data set of 187,602 black-owned enterprises in 1972 and 231,000 black-owned enterprises in 1977 -- thereby avoiding the response and selectivity bias so prevalent in previous work.

Chapter IV

AN ENTREPRENEURIAL DECISION MODEL OF FIRM FORMATION
AND FIRM CONTINUATION

The role of the entrepreneur appears to be of central importance to business formation and growth. The importance of this role for innovation, investment and active expansion of new markets, products and techniques has been emphasized by many investigators (Schumpeter,[1] Knight,[2] Leibenstein,[3] Kirzner,[4] Harris,[5] Baumol,[6] Leff,[7] and Davis[8]). The successful entrepreneur must display special aptitudes for bearing risk and uncertainty which permit him to act as a catalytic agent and promoter for new investment and production opportunities. This role in black business development seems especially critical since black entrepreneurs must not only shift and expand the opportunity set available to the community, but they must also often overcome unique problems of discrimination in capital markets and racial stereotypical attitudes of consumers in the product market. Viewed in these terms, entrepreneurship in the black-owned business sector is not simply a fourth factor of production, but a critical prerequisite for the securement and coordination of other productive services. Entrepreneurship as an alternative career choice for blacks is, therefore, the center piece of the theoretical framework in this chapter. Employment of other productive factors such as the hiring of labor and the acquisition and deployment of capital are seen as largely emanating from the entrepreneur's ability to successfully acquire and organize such productive resources.

With this premise, we formulate a model in three stages. The first stage analyzes the factors involved in choosing self-employment under no risk or uncertainty and their impact on firm formation and continuation. The second stage investigates factors involved in choosing self-employment under risk and uncertainty and their respective impact on employment size of firm, firm formation, and firm continuation. The last section investigates the impact of discrimination, both in acquiring resources and in product demand, on the likelihood of entry and continuation of black-owned firms.

All three stages of the model are concerned with entrepreneurial choice and the factors and potential obstacles which affect that choice vis-a-vis starting new ventures and continuing in business. As such, all three parts should be viewed as being complimentary. The first two parts, in particular, follow a certain sequence. The first stage isolates the essential elements of the self-employment decision and the implications of these fundamental factors on the likelihood of observing firm formations and successful firm continuations. In this first stage no explicit reference is made to either differences in risk aversion between individuals, or to differences in certainty of outcome or income receipt.

The second section extends the argument of the first section by explicitly comparing the expected utility of both exercising control of the firm and earning entrepreneurial income to the utility of a certain income stream earned in outside employment. This section is basically an adaptation of Kihlstrom and Laffont's entrepreneurial theory of firm formation based on risk aversion.[9] By explicity investigating expected utility functions, we are armed with a tool that enables us to explore the impact of risk and uncertainty on entrepreneurial choice and size of firms formed.

72

While Kihlstrom and Laffont's theory is very useful and suggestive, there are some limitations in the their approach revolving around, (i) their assumption of identical amounts of wealth to all individuals, (ii) no consideration to nonpecuniary benefits of self-employment, and (iii) their assumption that all individuals possess the same level of ability. Our model, on the other hand assumes different personal endowments of wealth, different levels of ability among individuals, and includes nonpecuniary benefits of ownership within the utility function.

The first two sections of the model jointly show that low endowments of personal wealth and the inability to generate sufficient amounts of retained earnings clearly inhibit the size of firms, the probability of forming new firms, and the success of existing firms to continue. This highlights the need for both access to external sources of capital and for increased opportunities to obtain higher levels of market demand. However, the ability to generate retained earnings from higher levels of product demand, and the ability to raise outside capital, is largely thwarted if discrimination results in an effective capital tariff, and in the withholding of demand for goods and services of the black entrepreneur. A model of black firm formation and continuation would be incomplete without an analysis of the impact of possible discrimination on the cost of doing business and on the ability to sell goods and services. This is done in the third section. While the first two sections focus on factors which impact entrepreneurial choice and on potential obstacles to entrepreneurial success, the degree and extent of which are mediated by the nature of entrepreneurship in the black community, the third section assesses a factor which is more unique to black entrepreneurs.

We assume that the entrepreneur's personal objective is similar to all other individuals: He seeks to maximize the present value of his standard-of-living by some terminal point T. In order to do so, however, he must sacrifice short-term, immediate consumption, in any given intermediate period t, in order to maximize the present value of his standard-of-living over the longer time horizon T. The entrepreneur, therefore, maximizes his terminal point standard-of-living by diverting some of his firm's earnings toward the purpose of increasing the net worth position of the firm. Using optimal control terminology, we can refer to entrepreneur's periodic withdrawals to support his consumption needs or standard-of-living as the control variable, and the growth in net worth of the firm as the state variable.

What is remarkable about this formulation is that by maximizing the discounted utility stream of the control variable by some terminal point T, subject to a state variable condition, one also maximizes the utility of the sum of the control and state variable at the steady-state, equilibrium point T. This property is well known from solutions to the classic Ramsey problem and from all optimal growth models of the firm and of the economy as a whole (see Ramsey,[10] Dorfman, Samuelson, and Solow,[11] Phelps,[12] Lancaster,[13] Burmeister and Dobell,[14] Koopmans,[15] and Jones[16]). Thus, when the entrepreneur maximizes the present value of his consumption stream subject to periodic investments of retained earnings to increase the value of the firm, he also maximizes the utility of the sum of his standard-of-living and the net worth of the firm at the terminal point. Therefore, the entrepreneur's objective can be equivalently stated in three alternative ways:

74

(i) By maximizing the present value of his standard-of-living utility stream, subject to a net worth or business savings constraint, the entrepreneur also,

(ii) maximizes the sum of his standard-of-living and own-firm net worth utility stream over time, subject to initial conditions, and also

(iii) maximizes the present value of the total expected income utility stream subject to cash withdrawals each period.

The entrepreneur can, therefore, be described as seeking to maximize the present value of his standard-of-living (C), where the total returns to the accumulated net worth in his own firm ($\hat{\imath}$ NW) are divided in any period t between investing in future additional net worth of the firm NW' (t) and in his own personal consumption, C (t). (Note that $\hat{\imath}$ is the rate of return on net worth). More formally, the entrepreneur seeks to,

(4.1) $\qquad$ Max $\int_0^T e^{-rt} U(C(t)) \, dt$

subject to, $\qquad \hat{\imath} \, NW(t) = NW'(t) + C(t)$

$\qquad$ or, $\qquad NW'(t) = \hat{\imath} \, NW(t) - C(t)$

Again, this is identical to choosing the path which produces the maximum utility stream (W) of personal consumption and net worth through time, where consumption at any time t+1 is a function of business savings and consumption decisions in period t. More formally this amounts to,

(4.2) $\qquad$ Max $\quad W(C(t), NW(t)) \, dt$

$\qquad$ = $\qquad$ Max $(W(C(1), NW(1)) + W(C(2), NW(2)), \ldots + W(C(T), NW(T)))$

subject to, $\qquad C(t+1) = f(C(t), NW(t))$

and given, $\bar{C}(0)$.

By expanding (4.1), subject to its constraints, we get,

(4.3) $\qquad \int_0^T e^{-rt} U(C(t)) \, dt = \int_0^T e^{-rt} U(\hat{\imath} \, NW(t) - NW'(t)) \, dt$

The Euler equation for this formulation is,

(4.4) $\quad\quad\quad\quad dF_{NW'}/dt = F_{NW}$

where,

(4.5) $\quad\quad\quad\quad F_{NW} = e^{-rt} U'(C) \hat{\imath}$

and,

(4.6) $\quad\quad\quad\quad F_{NW'} = -e^{-rt} U'(C)$

By substituting (4.5) and (4.6) into (4.4), we get

$$d(-e^{-rt} U'(C))/dt = e^{-rt} U'(C) \hat{\imath}$$

Thus, $\quad\quad\quad -e^{-rt} U''(C)C' + re^{-rt} U'(C) = e^{-rt} U'(C) \hat{\imath}$

Solving, we obtain

(4.7) $\quad -U''(C)C'/ U'(C) = \hat{\imath} - r$

Since $-U''(C)/ U'(C) > 0$ by assumption (i.e., $U'>0$, $U''<0$), the optimal solution is characterized by increasing consumption over time, $C' = dC/dt > 0$, if and only if $\hat{\imath} > r$. That is, the optimal standard-of-living path rises if the rate of return on the entrepreneur's personal net worth in the firm ($\hat{\imath}$) exceeds the enterpreneur's rate of impatience or rate of time perference (r). Moreover, the standard-of-living path is greater, the greater the difference between ($\hat{\imath}$) and (r). A relatively patient entrepreneur, with low rate of time preference, foregoes some current personal withdrawals from the firm to allow the value of the firm to improve so that a higher level of consumption and living standard may be obtained later.

The optimal solution satisfies both the basic equation $NW'(t) = \hat{\imath} NW(t) - C(t)$ and the Euler equation (4.4). To develop qualitative properties of the optimal solution, we construct a diagram in the non-negative C-NW plane. From (4.7), it is clear that $C' = 0$ when $\hat{i} = r$. Since $\hat{i}$ is monotone decreasing, $C' = dC/dt = 0$ has a unique solution $\hat{i} = f'(NW) = r$. Call this solution NW_s, and the $\hat{i}$ when $\hat{i} = r$, $\hat{i}_s$. If $NW > NW_s$, then $f'(NW) - r < f'(NW_s) - r = 0$, since $f'' < 0$ by the law of variable proportions. This can alternatively be written as $\hat{i} - r < \hat{i}_s - r = 0$. Hence from (4.7), since $-U''/U' > 0$ always, it follows that $C' < 0$ when $NW > NW_s$ and $\hat{i} - r < 0$. Similarly, $C' > 0$ when $NW < NW_s$. Therefore, to the right of NW_s, C must fall, and to the left of NW_s, C must rise. This is shown in Figure 4-a.

TABLE 4-a: DIRECTIONAL ARROWS FOR CHANGE IN CONSUMPTION

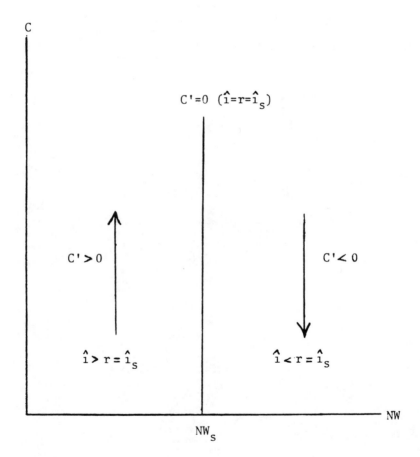

Next, since $NW' = \hat{i} NW - C$, whenever $C = \hat{i} NW$, then $NW' = 0$. The $NW' = 0$ curve described by $C = \hat{i} NW$, therefore, passes through the origin and has derivatives $dC/dNW = \hat{i} = f'(NW)$ 0, and $d^2C/dNW^2 = f''(NW)$ 0. This curve is, therefore, increasing and concave, and it cuts the NW-C plane into two regions. Following the general derivation of optimal control phase diagrams as outlined in Kamien and Schwartz[17], we can derive the remaining properties of the diagram: Let (NW_a, C_a) satisfy $C = \hat{i} NW$, when $NW' = 0$. Consider the point $(NW_a, C_a + m)$ where $m > 0$. Thus, $(NW_a, C_a + m)$ must be above (NW_a, C_a). From $NW' = \hat{i} NW - C$, it follows that $NW' = \hat{i} NW_a - (C_a + m) = -m < 0$; and so NW must be falling at $(NW_a, C_a + m)$. Therefore, NW is falling at every point above the $NW' = 0$ locus. Similarly, any point below the $NW' = 0$ locus $NW' > 0$, and NW must be rising. The directional arrows below reflect these conclusions. Figure 4-b indicates the general direction of movement that (NW,C) would take from any location. Note also that C is stationary along a path as the $C' = 0$ locus is crossed, and that NW is stationary as the $NW' = 0$ locus is crossed. (See Figure 4-b).

There is a steady - state level of firm net worth and standard-of-living that is sustainable. A steady-state position has $C' = 0$ and $NW' = 0$, where the optimal values of C and NW can be maintained indefinitely. This position occurs at (NW_s, C_s) where $C_s = f(NW_s)$. From the theorm regarding the existence of a solution to a differential equation, there is at most one path from the line $NW = NW_o$, the starting position, to the point (NW_s, C_s). (see Arrow and Kurz[18]; Intriligator[19]). Thus, we know in advance that there will be, at most, only one optimal path approaching (NW_s, C_s) from the left of NW_s, and, at most, only one optimal path approaching the sustainable steady-state solution (NW_s, C_s) from the right of NW_s.

TABLE 4-b: DIRECTIONAL ARROWS FOR CHANGE IN CONSUMPTION
AND NET WORTH

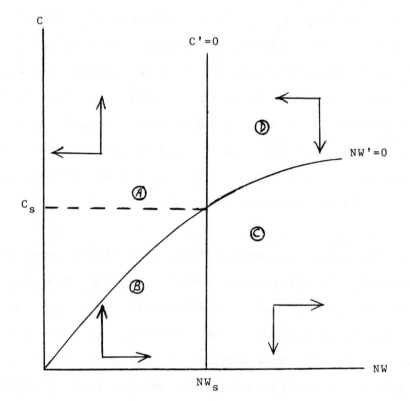

The exact nature of the optimal paths and the paths that are either infeasible or inferior is determined both by the rate of return or net worth ($\hat{i}$) relative to the entreprenur's given rate of time preference (r), and by the rate of return on net worth ($\hat{i}$) compared to that rate of return on net worth that can be sustained in the steady-state ($\hat{i}_s$). Thus, the nature of the paths describing the outcomes of entrepreneurial choice depends both on his willingness to reinvest in the firm, and the long run, sustainable rate of return dictated by the nature and extent of demand for his product or service. As long as the rate of return on net worth is greater than that in the steady-state, and simultaneously greater than the entrepreneur's rate of time preference (f'(NW) f'(NW$_s$), or $\hat{i} > \hat{i}_s$ = r), then personal consumption is increasing over time (C' > 0). In turn, net worth can either be increasing or decreasing, (NW'$\gtrless$0), depending on whether consumption withdrawals (C) out of total returns to net worth of the firm ($\hat{i}$ NW) are sufficiently moderate or too large. The first case where $\hat{i}$ >r and C > $\hat{i}$ NW is shown in Figure 4-b as area Ⓐ where C is increasing and NW is falling. The second case where $\hat{i} < \hat{i}_s$ = r, and C < $\hat{i}$ NW is shown as area Ⓑ in Figure 4-b, where both C and NW are increasing continuously over time.

All paths in area Ⓐ are inferior to those in Ⓑ since ever increasing levels of consumption withdrawals are too large and cannot be sustained indefinitely with net worth continuously falling and ultimately crossing into NW < 0, an infeasible region. All paths in Ⓑ are superior to all paths in Ⓐ since both consumption withdrawals and firm net worth are increasing there in every period. However, only one such path in Ⓑ will be optimal.

All paths in Ⓒ are also inferior to those in Ⓑ since the discounted utility stream of the sum of consumption and net worth cannot be maximized at the terminal point given that the standard-of-living (consumption) is falling continuously over time. Here, even though withdrawals are less than the returns to the firm, resulting in the growth of net worth, the rate of return on net worth is continuously falling below that required for steady-state equilibrium. Net worth is being heedlessly increased, in this case, despite lower and lower rates of return and declining standard-of-living.

All paths in area $\textcircled{D}$ also have net worth levels in excess of the sustainable, steady-states level of net worth (NW_s). Likewise, consumption levels in $\textcircled{D}$ exceed the steady-state consumption (C_s). The discounted utility stream of higher net worth and higher consumption levels would be preferable, but all such paths are unstable since the rate of return is both less than the entrepreneur's rate of time preference and less than that, therefore, required in the steady-state. In addition, consumption withdrawals continuously exceed the declining returns, thereby further depressing net worth in future periods, such that $NW' < 0$. Consequently, both total net worth and total consumption must fall continuously over time. Only one such path in $\textcircled{D}$, however, will optimally approach the steady-state solution from above. All other paths veer off either into inferior region $\textcircled{A}$, where the entrepreneur seeks to reclaim his fallen standard-of-living by continuously depressing firm net worth, or into inferior region $\textcircled{C}$, where the entrepreneur tries to expand firm net worth in the face of continuously declining rates of return and declining living standards.

It follows, from the reasoning above that if initial firm net worth $N\bar{W}_s$ is less than the steady-state solution, then the approach to (NW_s, C_s) must be from below with NW and C both increasing monotonically from their initial values to their stationary values along unique path $\textcircled{1}$ (Figure 4-c).

TABLE 4-c: OPTIMAL PATHS OF CONSUMPTION AND NET WORTH

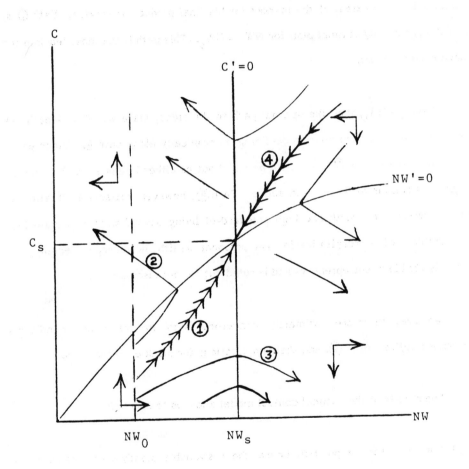

If the initial amount of withdrawals for personal consumption is too large (as in path ②), then net worth could only be accumulated for a short while and eventually diminish to the point where eventually net worth could ultimately cross into NW < 0, an infeasible solution. If, on the other hand, initial consumption withdrawals were chosen too low, then consumption would increase in later periods and peak, and then decline, as shown in path ③. This case would occur if the entrepreneur were trying to increase the value of the firm beyond what was warranted by the extent of the market for his final product or service. Path ① is, therefore, the only optimal plan for $NW_o < NW_s$. This path is the most feasible for black entrepreneurs.

If $NW_o > NW_s$, then the optimal path to the steady state would have both net worth and personal consumption declining montonically along path ④. Other paths in the neighborhood of ④ can, again, be ruled out as either infeasible or inferior by arguments similar to those cited above. Path ④, however, reflects a situation of both excessive net worth and high standard-of-living beyond what is sustainable. This problem of overcapitalization via personal wealth, however, is certainly an anomaly for black entrepreneurs and is ruled out for our discussion.

We are, therefore, primarily concerned with the necessary conditions describing optimal path ①, and their implications for black entrepreneurs.

The results of the optimal control model allow us to conclude.

(i) For any starting position below the sustainable steady-state standard-of-living/net worth position, the only optimal path for black entrepreneurs is the path of both increasing net worth to the firm and increasing standard-of-living.

(ii) This optimal path rises if and only if the rate of return on net worth ($\hat{i}$) exceeds th entrepreneur's rate of time preference (r). Consequently, the more impatient (patient) the entrepreneur, the lower (higher) the likelihood of continuing in business, and under a rational choice model, the less (more) desirable it is for him to start a business.

(iii) A necessary condition for movement along the optimal standard-of-living/net worth path is that the market demand for the entrepreneur's product must be large enough to obtain a rate of return on net worth ($\hat{i}$) greater than the long run sustainable rate of return in the steady state ($\hat{i}_s$) over T-1 periods.

(iv) The standard-of-living path and the value of the entrepreneur's income stream are greater the greater the difference between $\hat{i}$ and r. It follows that the greater his previous investment in human capital, the greater the gap between $\hat{i}$ and r for two reasons. First, returns to investment in the firm ($\hat{i}$) are higher the greater the past accumulation of knowledge and experience of the individual. Second, the rate of impatience or time preference (r) is lower for individuals with larger amounts of human capital since they have already demonstrated a willingness to postpone current income and invest for future returns.

Opportunity Costs of Self-Employment

The conditions required to maximize the present value of the income stream, or the discounted utility stream, to self-employment while critically important in their own right, do not, by themselves, give a complete theory of entrepreneurial choice under certainty. To complete the picture we must explicitly consider the opportunity costs of self-employment compared to other career choices.

Minimizing opportunity costs entails individuals choosing the career choice offering the greatest returns.

Let a potential black entrepreneur's total return on general education and training measured in terms of value of output, applicable anywhere, be represented by GHC (general human capital), and his firm specific human capital by FHC. The value of output per unit of FHC is $(m+n)$, where m measures the expected rate of return to the black entrepreneur's own -firm per unit of specific human captial, and n is a random variable with a density function $\phi(n)$, with $E(n) = 0$. While m is seen as specific to the entrepreneur's own-firm, n can be thought of as reflecting demand changes and fluctuations which deviate from "normal" or expected market conditions for his product or service, hence the reason $E(n) = 0$. As such, n reflects the actual impact of exogenous factors on the derived demand for the factor of production, entrepreneurship. Such exogenous factors include cyclical fluctuations, the degree or change in taste for the product or service, and the number of substitutes or competitors. We let E be the value per unit of FHC in the alternative employment of working for a majority firm. We note by assumption that $Cov(n, E) = 0$; that is, we do not expect demand fluctuations for self-employed output to be especially correlated with his (her) value in alternative employment opportunities.

Setting consumption withdrawals $C(t)$ equal to the amount of self-remuneration from entrepreneurship (W_{se}), the value of the entrepreneur to his or her own-firm in any period (t) is given by,

(4.8)
$$V_{se}(t) = GHC + (m(t) + n(t))\, FHC = C(t) + NW'(t)$$
$$= W_{se}(t) + NW'(t)$$

Note, of course, that the value of the entrepreneur to his or her own-firm is identical to the total returns to net worth in any period t.

The value in <u>alternative employment</u> V_{alt} is given by,

(4.9) $\qquad V_{alt}(t) = GHC + \mathcal{E}(t)FHC = W(t)$

The quasi-rent (R) to entrepreneurial specific capital is, therefore,

(4.10) $\qquad R(t) = V_{se}(t) - Valt(t) = (m(t) - n(t) - \mathcal{E}(t)) \, FHC$

For values of $R(t) > 0$, self-employment is preferred; for values of $R(t) < 0$, the best alternative career is preferred. For $R(t) = 0$, the opportunity cost fo self-employment is exactly covered by the next best alternative, and the person is indifferent between outside employment and owning their own business. More specifically, quasi - rent (R) is zero when $n = 0$. That is, the entrpreneur "breaks even" when normal profits are earned and the opportunity costs of self-employment are exactly covered. In this case,

(4.11) $\qquad R(t) = V_{se}(t) - Valt(t) = (m(t) - \mathcal{E}(t)) \, FHC = 0$, when $n = 0$.

In this case, the rate of return to the entrepreneur's own-firm (m) per unit of specific captial is equal to the value per unit of specific capital in alternative employment $\mathcal{E}$. If we assume that this amount is equal to what is required for sustaining one's standard-of-living, then $NW'(t) \gtreqless 0$ as $n \gtreqless 0$. This is reflected below in Figure 4-d.

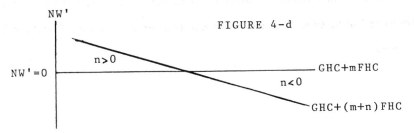

FIGURE 4-d

87

While little can be said concerning the required number of periods for which n(t) must be negative before a career shift is undertaken, it is clear that the probability of self-employment P(SE) is greater for values of $R(t) > 0$, with n(t) and $NW(t) > 0$ than for values of $R(t) < 0$ with $n(t) < 0$ and $NW(t) < 0$. That is,

(4.12) $P(SE/R(t)>0) > P(SE/R(t)<0) \Longrightarrow P(SE/n(t)>0) > P(SE/n(t)<0)$.

Hypotheses Emerging from Self-Employment Under Certainty

(1) Higher levels of education, business knowledge, and business experience increase the probability of black-owned firms forming and continuing in business. Thus, areas with higher median black education and longer traditions of black business ownership should experience relatively greater formation rates and lower rates of failure.

(2) With any given level of business savings behavior (reflecting the entrepreneur's rate of time preference), higher levels of market demand for products and services of black-owned firms should increase the rate of return on business net worth— thereby lowering firm failure and encouraging firm formations.

(3) Fluctuations in market conditions impact fluctuations in business net worth. Black-owned firm formations and continuations are, therefore, directly related to the business cycle and to upward fluctuations in the level of demand. Likewise, black-owned firm failures are inversely associated with the business cycle and to downward fluctuations in the level of demand for black-owned firms' products and services.

(4) Factors which increase the payment for outside, alternative employment to black professionals and managers over self-employment remuneration decrease the likelihood of the formation of new ventures, and decrease (increase) the likelihood of continuations (failures) in black business ownership.

(5) For any given level of remuneration from self-employment, factors which are associated with lower professional and managerial alternative opportunities for blacks increase the likelihood of formations of new ventures and increase (decrease) likelihood of continuations (failures) in black business ownership.

SELF-EMPLOYMENT UNDER RISK AND UNCERTAINTY

While the riskless alternative wage can be estimated with some certainty, even under conditions where it is not fixed and allowed to fluctuate, remuneration for self-employment is a purely stochastic payment derived essentially from owning and operating a risky firm. In fact, the role of the entrepreneur and his claim to the net returns of the business is largely based on his being rewarded for accepting the risk and uncertainty of personal reward. According to Schumpeter this reward is the payment for undertaking the role of being an innovator, of organizing and coordinating factors of production with previously unutilized or underutilized inventions in new ways. Under Knight, the entrepreneur receives payment for the risk of not working at a riskless wage. The entrepreneur in this formulation bears the risks associated with securing the owners of productive services against uncertainty and fluctuation in their incomes. (See also Baily[20] and Azariadis[21] for this concept employed in implicit contract theory).

The model thus far, therefore, has three shortcomings: (1) It does not incorporate differences in risk aversion among individuals choosing between self-employment and outside employment, (2) It does not explore the full implications of uncertainty arising from external factors, and (3) It does not allow for nonpecuniary benefits associated with owning one's own business -- whereby even if the self-paid remuneration were somewhat less than the alternative wage, an individual might still rationally choose self-employment. We, therefore, extend our basic approach by assuming that for each firm there is an expected utility maximizing entrepreneur who makes decisions and, in Knight's language, exercises responsible control of the business. An expected utility function can incorporate these nonpecuniary benefits and risk factors. Similar to Knight, we define the entrepreneur as the owner-operator of the business who accepts the risk.

Consistent with the choice theoretic framework discussed previously, individuals are assumed to have a choice between owning and operating a risky firm or working for a riskless wage. Consequently, it is reasonable to conjecture that less risk averse individuals become entrepreneurs, while more risk averse individuals work for entrepreneurs who tend to assume such risks. We now, therefore, define the opportunity costs of self-employment as the certainty utility foregone by undertaking entrepreneurial activities instead of working as an employee. Conversely, the opportunity cost of being a worker is the expected utility foregone by being an employee instead of an entrepreneur.

In developing the properties of this version of the model, we adopt and follow very closely the work of Kihlstrom and Laffont[22] regarding their entrepreneurial theory of firm formation based on risk aversion. There are, however, some important differences. Like Kihlstrom and Laffont, we assume that individuals differ in their willingness to bear risks; but we do not assume, as they do, that individuals are the same in their ability to perform entrepreneurial functions and outside labor. It should be clear from our previous discussion that we assume individuals do differ in ability and aptitude. The model, however, is consistent with our assumption that the distribution of individual abilities is identical among all ethnic and racial groups. We assert this as an axiom. Second, we also assume that wealth differs among individuals, whereas Kihlstrom and Laffont assume everyone has an identical amount of wealth. This assumption seems to be particularly restrictive in generating implications for black entrepreneurs who have significantly low endowments of personal wealth. Third, as previously alluded to in the first section, our model incorporates the impact of external, state-of-nature shocks which cause deviations from normal market conditions. Lastly, we also include nonpecuniary income in our model.

General Equilibrium Conditions:

Following Kihlstrom and Laffont, we define a set of agents within the interval $(0,1)$. If α $(0,1)$, individual α has the Von Neumann - Morgenstern utility function $U(I, \alpha)$, where I represents in our model both total money income from self-employment (π) and nonpecuniary income (S), and where $I \varepsilon (0, \infty)$. That is, the entrepreneur seeks to maximize the present value of I such that,

(4.13) $\qquad \int_o^T e^{-rt} I(t) = \int_o^T e^{-rt} (\pi(t) + S(t))$, where, $\pi = \hat{1} \, NW$, as previously defined.

For all $I(t) \gtrless 0$, the first and second derivatives U' and U" exist and are continuous. The marginal utility U' is positive and nonincreasing, i.e., $U" \leq 0$. Thus, all agents are either risk averse, to varying degrees, or indifferent to risk (risk neutral).

We employ the customary Arrow-Pratt absolute risk aversion measure which is nondecreasing in α. If α is more risk averse than agent β, or at least as risk averse as β then by definition,

(4.14) $\qquad r(I,\alpha) = -U''(I,\alpha)/U'(I,\alpha) \geqslant -U''(I,\beta)/U'(I,\beta) = r(I,\beta)$

for all I $(0,\infty)$.

As we have already indicated, individuals have a choice of becoming entrepreneurs and receiving an uncertain income, or they can work and receive the market wage, w. If an individual α becomes an entrepreneur and employs L workers, he will receive profits equal to,

(4.15) $\qquad \pi(w,\alpha) = g(L,e,n) - wL(w,\alpha)$

where $g(L,e,n)$ is a continuous production function whose arguments are labor (L), entrepreneurial skill (e), and a random parameter n representing deviations from the normal state of market demand (state of nature), with $E(n) = 0$.

Each individual α has a given amount of accumulated savings and wealth, $H(\alpha)$, which varies across individuals, such that certain agents are unable to hire workers if $H(\alpha) = 0$. We are, therefore, employing a type of wage-fund theory where labor-hiring must be less than or equal to $H(\alpha)/w$:.

(4.16) $\qquad L(w,\alpha) \leq H(\alpha)/w$

Consequently, possession of wealth constitutes a necessary condition for generating a new firm with paid employees. However, it is not sufficient, in itself, since other factors including the type of business and expected level of sales must be considered.

An individual $\propto$ who becomes an entrepreneur, therefore, will employ $L(w,\propto)$ workers where $L(w, \propto)$ is the L value in $(0, H(\propto)/w)$ which maximizes the expected utility function,

(4.17) $\qquad$ $EU(H(\propto) + g(L,e,n) - wL(w,\propto), S(\propto))$

If either $U'' < 0$, or $g'' < 0$, which is customarily assumed, then L is unique. By (4.15) we know that $\not\! \Pi = g(L, e, n) - wL$. It follows, then, that individual $\propto$ will choose or be indifferent to being an entrepreneur when

(4.18) $\qquad$ $EU(H(\propto) + \not\! \Pi(w,\propto), S(\propto)) \gtrless U(H(\propto) + w)$

And he will choose or be indifferent to being an employee and work at wage w if

(4.19) $\qquad$ $EU(H(\propto) + \not\! \Pi (w,\propto), S(\propto)) \lesssim U(H(\propto) + w)$

He will be indifferent if the equality in (4.18) and (4.19) holds.

Equilibrium is reached in this system when the labor market clears. At the equilibrium wage, labor demanded by all agents who choose to become entrepreneurs equals that supplied by agents who choose to enter the labor market. The formal proof that equilibrium exists is essentially the same as Kihlstrom and Laffont, and is not reproduced here.

A number of properties can be derived upon defining a <u>certainty equivalent wage</u>. In the previous discussion this certainty equivalent wage existed along the q=o line, where the remuneration for self-employment equalled the marginal product, and hence the riskless wage, of alternative employment. Here the <u>certainty equivalent wage $w(\propto)$</u> is again that market wage which makes agent

$\propto$ indifferent between the two activities -- work and entrepreneurship -- and is defined by

(4.20) $\qquad$ $EU\big(H(\propto) + \not\! \Pi(w(\propto), \quad S(\propto)\big) = U\big(H(\propto) + w(\propto)\big)$

Given $g'' < 0$ and $U'' < 0$, the following properties emerge from the model,

(i) For each $\alpha \in (0,1)$

$$EU\big(H(\alpha) + \tilde{\pi}(w,\alpha), S(\alpha)\big) - U(H(\alpha) + w)$$

is a continuous monotonically decreasing function of w. That is, for any agent α higher riskless market wages decrease the net utility of self-employment over employee status, and increase the utility of working compared to entrepreneurship.

(ii) $w(\alpha)$ is a well-defined function of α, meaning for each $\alpha \in (0,1)$, $w(\alpha)$ exists and is unique; and in addition $w(\alpha) > 0$.

(iii) If $w > (<) w(\alpha)$, then $EU\big(H(\alpha) + \tilde{\pi}(w,\alpha), S(\alpha)\big) < (>) U(H(\alpha) + w)$

This is an extension of (i) and says that if the market wage exceeds (is less than) the certainty equivalent wage for α, then the expected utility of entrepreneurship for α is less than (exceeds) the certain utility from working for others.

(iv) If $r(I,\alpha) > r(I,\beta)$, then $w(\alpha) < w(\beta)$

That is, if α is <u>more</u> risk averse than β, then α requires a lower certainty equivalent wage in order to choose employee status. More risk averse individuals are induced to become workers at lower wages than less risk averse (greater risk taking) agents.

(v) If $r(I,\beta) > (<) r(I,\alpha)$,

then $\qquad EU\big(H(\beta) + \tilde{\pi}(w(\alpha)), S(\beta),\beta\big) < (>) U\big(H(\beta) + w(\alpha),\beta\big)$

Given that the ruling market wage is the certainty equivalent wage of α , and that, therefore, α is the marginal entrepreneur, this result states that all individuals, who are more (less) risk averse than the marginal entrepreneur will be workers (entrepreneurs). This result also implies that there will always be some equilibrium wage for which there are marginal entrepreneurs.

The monotonicity property plus property (iii) allow us to to construct Figure 4-e.

TABLE 4-e: RISK AVERSION AND THE DECISION TO BECOME
AN ENTREPRENEUR

E(U),U

DECISION
TO BECOME
AN ENTREPRENEUR

U(H(α)+W)

EU(H(α)+$\bar{\pi}$(W,α),S(α))

W(α)

W

We now assume that differences in wealth lead to differences in degree of risk aversion. More specifically, we assume that individuals of type a with greater wealth have less risk averse utility functions than β-type individuals with lower wealth.

That is,

(4.21) $H(\alpha) > H(\beta) \Longrightarrow -U''(H(\alpha), I(\alpha)) / U'(H(\alpha), I(\alpha)) < -U''(H(\beta), I(\beta)) / U'(H(\beta), I(\beta))$

or more directly,

(4.22) $H(\alpha) > H(B) \Longrightarrow r(H(\alpha), I(\alpha)) < r(H(\beta), I(\beta))$

Note that this assumption is somewhat less stringent than the Friedman-Savage assumption of utility functions changing direction accross wealth-income categories, whereby the utiltiy map is concave at low incomes, convex at middle incomes, and concave again at high incomes (Figure 4-f). Here we are simply assuming that potential entrepreneurs with low personal financial assets are more risk averse than wealthier individuals, such that their expected utility functions are more concave than the utility functions of wealthier entrepreneurs (Figure 4-g).

FIGURE 4-f: RISK AVERSENESS AND WEALTH, FRIEDMAN-SAVAGE HYPOTHESIS

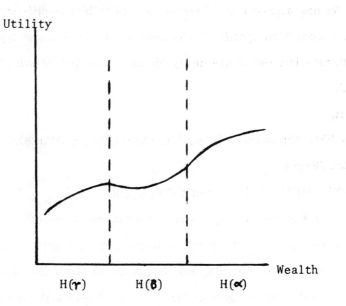

FIGURE 4-g: RISK AVERSENESS AND WEALTH, THESIS ASSUMPTION

$$H(\alpha) > H(\beta) \implies r(H(\alpha)) < r(H(\beta))$$

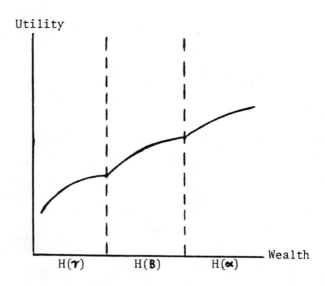

Since by assumption poorer individuals are more risk averse than wealthier individuals it than follows from the initial equilibrium conditions that,

(1) Poorer individuals are induced to become workers, and refrain from entrepreneurial activity, at lower market wages than wealthier individuals. (property iv)

(2) Given a ruling certainty equivalent wage $W(\beta)$, such that β is the marginal entrepreneur, all individuals who are wealthier and therefore less risk averse than the marginal entrepreneur will be entrepreneurs. (property v)

(3) Given a ruling certainty equivalent wage $W(\beta)$, such that β is the marginal entrepreneur, all individuals who are poorer and therefore more risk averse than the marginal entrepreneur will be workers. (also via property v)

Personal wealth is seen here as also including personal access to family financial assets and investment funds from friends. Thus, we should also expect individuals from higher income families and higher income communities to have greater willingness to start new ventures of greater size as compared to individuals from poorer families and poorer communities.

To summarize, since wealth (H) varies across individuals, it follows from our assumption and subsequent discussion that the most risk averse individuals will be the poorest initially, and that these individuals will be associated with the lowest financial asset-holding communities and families. Additionally, relatively greater risk - takers, _ceteris paribus,_ are wealthier and will be associated with families and communties endowed with higher financial assets. We should therefore expect that groups or communities with the least financial assets will have the lowest rates of business formation; and that the distribution of those firms that are formed will be skewed toward the smallest sized firms. The net result will be that such persons and communities will derive the lowest benefit from business participation (Figure 4-h).

FIGURE 4-h: RISK AVERSENESS, WEALTH, AND SIZE AND NUMBER OF FIRMS

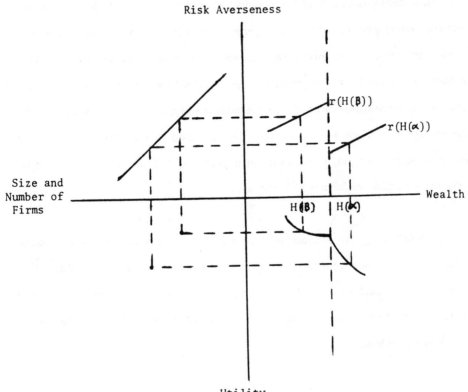

Comparative Statics:

The previous sections outlined the general equilibrium conditions regarding entrepreneurial choice under personal risk aversion. These conditions were then used to generate properties concerning the impact of differences in wealth endowments among individual entrepreneurs. Personal wealth constitutes an endogenous factor which varies across agents at any point in time. As such, the previous section is not explicitly designed to generate, by itself, any conclusions or hypotheses concerning the impact of exogenous factors on firm formations, failures, or continuations over any two discrete points in time. In the the following section, therefore, we utilize the general equilibrium results of the previous section to compare an initial equilibrium position with subsequent equilibrium positions resulting from exogenous changes in economy - wide or area - wide risk (changes in the state-of-nature). Such exogenous changes in area - wide risk, from the entrepreneur's point of view, may be reflected in such things as substantial swings in local unemployment, shifts in population, and the influx or outflight of substantial number of industries in the area.

The following two propositions are assumed to be valid since their proofs as theorms, similar in content to the lemmas expressed here, are given in Baron[23] and Kihlstrom and Laffont[24]. These lemmas are stated in a form useful for our purposes and are used to demonstrate certain important properties also shown in the diagrams below.

Lemma 1:

If $r(H(\alpha), I(\alpha))_t > (<) r(H(\alpha), I(\alpha))_0$ for every I, then $L_t(w,\alpha)$ is lower (higher) at every w than was $L_0(w,\alpha)$.

This means that increases in economy-wide risk reduce the amount of workers hired, and that decreases in economy-wide risk increase the amount of workers hired.

By lemma (1), it follows that factors which increase risk and uncertainty induce firms to use less labor (i.e., smaller sized firms). This implies fewer firms with paid employees and greater number of firms with no paid employees as r(I) rises for all I. (Note this is not a change in the shape of the risk averse schedule but a <u>shift</u> of a given schedule due to the impact of external factors for each and every entrepreneurial income I (Figure 4-i).

FIGURE 4-i: CHANGE IN ECONOMY-WIDE RISK AND SIZE OF FIRM

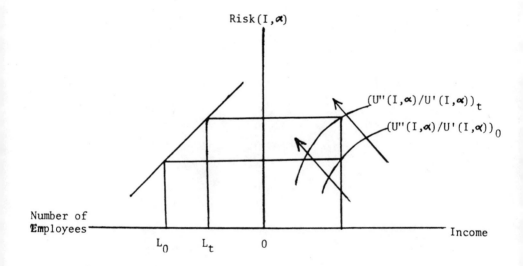

<u>Lemma 2:</u>

If $r\big(H(\alpha), I(\alpha)\big)_t > (<) r\big(H(\alpha), I(\alpha)\big)_0$ for every I, then

$$EU\big(H(\alpha) + \tilde{\pi}(w,\alpha), S(\alpha)\big)_t < (>) EU\big(H(\alpha) + \tilde{\pi}(w,\alpha), S(\alpha)\big)_0$$

This means that increasing economy-wide risk reduces the expected utility from entrepreneurship, and that decreasing economy-wide risk increases the expected utility from entrepreneurship.

Since increases in economy-wide risk decrease the expected utility from entrepreneurship, it follows that increased risk is associated with a decrease in the number of individuals deciding to become entrepreneurs. It will also, equivalently, lower the certainty equivalent wage at which individuals will choose employee status in alternative employment. (See Figure 4-j).

TABLE 4-j: CHANGE IN ECONOMY-WIDE RISK AND THE
DECISION TO BECOME AN ENTERPRENEUR

(Given: $r(H(\alpha))_t > r(H(\alpha))_0$)

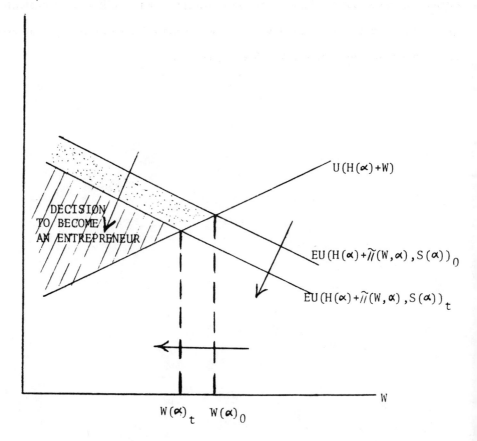

Differences in Uncertainty Across Geographic Areas

We have seen that upward shifts in the Arrow-Pratt absolute risk aversion function over two points in time represent an increase in risk for all persons in every income or wealth category. We also postulated that such shifts are impacted by a number of environmental factors which may exist in any given geographical area. Possible factors conjectured to impact changes in the state-of-nature included changes in the business cycle, abrupt population changes or shifts, changes in industrial composition and development, alterations in the tax-base and other changes in market conditions. It would seem to follow immediately that differences in such factors across geographical areas would also be significantly linked to differences in risk and uncertainty across these areas. Thus, a diagram could easily be constructed which would show that areas having higher levels of actual and perceived risk and uncertainty are associated with lower firm formations smaller firm sizes, and higher number of firm failures.

Under this prospect, all of the factors collectively impacting the degree of risk across areas would, therefore, also simultaneously impact the percent of those in the population choosing self-employment across these places. This also follows immediately from the general equilibrium model since greater risk and uncertainty results in individuals choosing employment over entrepreneurial pursuits at lower certainty eqivalent wages. Consequently, areas with more individuals possessing lower personal risk aversion, and lower area-wide perceived risk, must, under the model, have greater number of entrepreneurs (persons self-employed) per unit of population. Differences in the percent of those choosing self-employment, therefore, is a good proxy for differences in perceived risk and uncertainty across geographical areas.

<u>Expected Impacts Emerging from Self-Employment Under Risk</u>

1.   Groups and communities with the least amount financial assets will have the lowest rates of firm formation and the highest rates of firm discontinuation.

2.   Since income is both a determinant of personal risk aversion and a prime source of savings, individuals from higher income families and communities have a greater ability to start new ventures than do poorer individuals from lower income families and communities.

3.   Higher unemployment and other environmental factors which increase area-wide risk and uncertainty lower firm formations and the likelihood of observing firms with paid employees.

4.   Differences in the state-of-nature (environmental risk) across geographical areas impact the entrepreneurial decision -- resulting in differences in formation and continuation rates across geographical areas.

DISCRIMINATION AS A BARRIER-TO-ENTRY AND CONTINUATION

<u>Efffect of Discrimination on Black Firms' Cost Curves</u>

It is important to reemphasize that all the previous factors discussed concerning entrepreneurial choice to start firms apply equally well in explaining entrepreneurial choice to continue in business. In this same vein, barriers-to-entry, in general, and discrimination against minority entrepreneurs, in particular, can impact entrepreneurs in two ways: (1) they can deter potential entrants at the outset and (2) they can prevent or damper the success of those who do enter. (This usage is now standard in the barrier-to-entry literature, see Yip,[23] Caves,[24] Gupta,[25] Weiss,[26] and Needham[27]. The discussion that follows concerning discrimination as a barrier-to-entry, therefore, applies equally to probability of entry and likelihood of continuance.

Previous models of discrimination (Becker,[28] Thurow,[29] Arrow,[30] Kruger [31]) have primarily centered around the impact of discrimination on one or more of the following, (1) black worker employment or unemployment, (2) black and white wage levels, (3) black and white returns to capital, (4) comparative human capital investment between black and white workers; (5) occupational choice among workers. Item three (3) comes closest to our area of consideration, with the received theory in this area resting largely on the work of Becker and Thurow.

It will be of some benefit to our model to quickly review their views in this area. In Becker's work discrimination is a restrictive practice that interrupts free trade between two societies, white and black. If free trade existed, black society would export labor (its relatively abundant factor) and white society would export capital (its relatively abundant factor) until the value of labor and the marginal product of capital were the same for both races everywhere. Consistent with this framework, Becker derives the conclusion that discrimination, by disrupting free trade, decreases black wages and returns to white capital while increasing return to white labor and black capital. Given that labor is the relatively abundant factor for blacks and that capital is the relatively abundant factors for whites, the inference is drawn that incomes for both groups probably fall due to discrimination against blacks. Thurow finds Becker's conclusions of (1) lower living standards for whites, (2) lower returns on white capital and (3) higher returns to black capital due to discrimination to be seriously at odds with empirical observation. For Thurow, economic and social discrimination not only prevents blacks from importing white capital but it forces the export of black capital away from their communities to where effective tariffs do not exist and returns are greater. In sum, Thurow concludes that discrimination forces the black community to export its productive factors and import its consumption goods.

We adopt Thurow's assumptions that capital discrimination, occupational discrimination, and barriers to access to human capital effectively lower returns to black capital. This is consistent with blacks having restricted access to external sources of capital funds as well as their paying a premium on funds they are able to borrow. White capital on the other hand, can only lose from discrimination if rates of return in the black society exceeds that in the white society, which is ruled out by clear empirical evidence.

For our purposes we will define barrriers-to-entry as all obstacles outside the control of the firm which raise the cost curves of the firm to such an extent that it prevents or curtails new firms from producing a particular category of good or service profitably. In our model, then, discrimination clearly imposes a discrimination coefficient (tariff) on the cost of doing business by black entrepreneurs. This tariff is not only reflected in capital premiums and in other restrictions to capital, but also in socially restricted access to (1) information and knowledge available to the majority business sector, (2) supplies and materials at preferred customer rates, (3) equitable insurance rates, and (4) bonding availability.

A total cost function without discrimination barriers can be expressed as

110

(4.23) $C = cq + k$, where q = output; k = fixed costs; and c = variable costs.

We specify a linear demand curve,

(4.24) $P = a - bq$

The profit maximizing entrepreneur would therefore seek to maximize,

$$\pi = TR - TC = PQ - TC = (aq - bq^2) - (cq + k)$$

solving for $d\pi/dQ = 0$ we obtain profit maximizing output as, $q = (a-c)/2b$

at profit maximizing price, $p = (a + c)/2$

Thus, in a nondiscriminatory world profit maximization depends solely on "c" the marginal cost of production and "a" the y intercept or level demand.

Discrimination, however, as a barrier-to-entry changes the profit maximizing output level (q*) and price (p*). By assumption, we hold the demand curve constant and investigate its impact on the cost structure. The total cost function is now subject to a tariff (d),

(4.25) $C(1+d) = (cq* + k)(1+d)$

Profit maximizing conditions now give us

(4.26) $q* = (a - c - dc)/2b$ and $p* = (a + c + dc)/2$

Consequently, in a world of discrimination, output is lower ($q* < q$) and prices are higher ($p* > p$) for the discriminated entrepreneur. This reflected in an upward shift of the marginal cost curve by the vertical distance "dc" (Figure 4-k).

111

TABLE 4-k: IMPACT OF DISCRIMINATION ON PRICING
AND OUTPUT

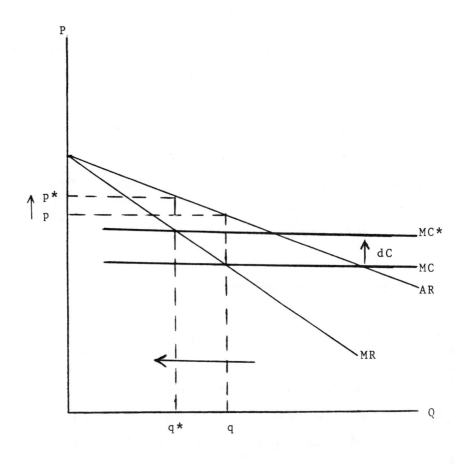

We can reasonably assume the Sylos postulate (see Sylos-Labini[32], and Needham[33]) that potential entrants behave as though they expect existing producers in an industry to maintain their output at the pre-entry level in the face of entry, and that established firms do, in fact, behave in this manner if entry occurs. Since the output from black-owned businesses is so small a fraction of total output in every industry, this is an eminently reasonable assumption for our model.

Given the Sylos postulate, black entrepreneurs are confronted by a sloping demand curve which is the segment of the industry demand curve to the right of the pre-entry quantity produced by existing firms. Entrepreneurs must decide whether to enter or remain in business by comparing this demand curve to their own cost conditions, which must include the opportunity costs of being self-employed.

To be more precise, the presence of discrimination offers a <u>potential</u> barrier since discrimination by itself is not sufficient to guarantee an operative barrier to entry. Entry and continuance can occur despite discrimination <u>if</u> the entrepreneur's anticipated or actual demand conditions result in a situation where profits can be made over and above the <u>full</u> <u>average</u> <u>cost</u> (inclusive of the discrimination tariff and opportunity costs of self-employment). Entry and continuance will <u>not occur</u> if the black entrepreneur's price exceeds cost in established firms by less than the difference between the full average cost of the black entrepreneur and that of established firms—for under this circumstance the entrepreneur's anticipated demand curve will be below his full cost curve. This difference is measured by the xy distance in Figure 4-1. If the discrimination tariff (d) raises the full average total cost curve for black firms too much (distance dc)

TABLE 4-1: ENTRY AND CONTINUATION UNDER NO DISCRIMINATION

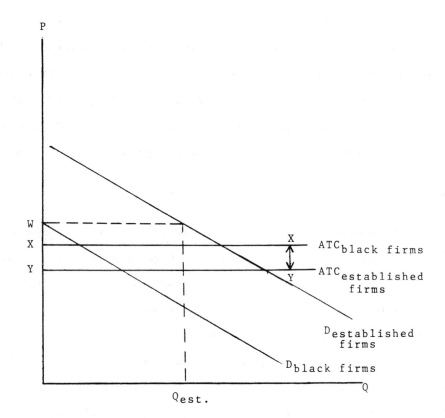

NOTE: Successful entry and continuation can occur when
black firms' price can be set above X in the WX
range, which is above the XY difference.

neither successful entry or continuation is possible. (Cases of successful entrance and continuation are shown in Figure 4-l, while the cases of no successful entry or continuation are shown in Figure 4-m). Consequently, entrepreneurs drawn from an identifiable group which labors under social and economic discrimination will have inefficient production (lower output at higher prices), and lower likelihood of successful start-ups and continuations.

TABLE 4-m: ENTRY AND CONTINUATION UNDER DISCRIMINATION

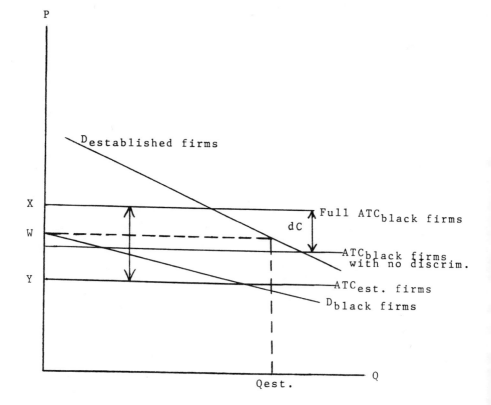

NOTE: No entry or continuation is feasible since black
firms' price can only be established within the
WY range, at best, which is less than the XY
difference.

Discrimination in the Market for Black Entrepreneurial Output

Discrimination, of course, not only affects the cost structure of black-owned firms, but also the market for goods and services produced by such firms. No elaborate demonstration is needed to show that its effect on any given entrepreneurial demand curve is to shift it down in the southwest direction. Given that the black firms' demand curve in Figure 4-n will shift down even further in the southwest direction due to discrimination in the market, black entrepreneurs price will be in even further below their full cost curve than was true previously. Thus, the effect of discrimination on both the supply and demand functions of black-owned firms reinforce lower probability of successful entry and continuation.

TABLE 4-n: DISCRIMINATION FOR BLACK ENTERPRENEURIAL
PRODUCTS AND SERVICES

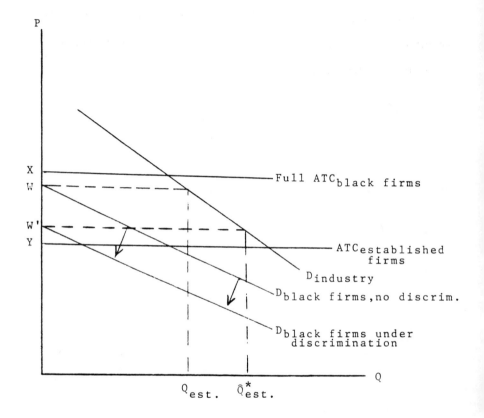

NOTE: Amount of market unavailable to black firms due
to market discrimination is shown by difference
between Q^*_{est} and Q_{est}.

SUMMARY:

The decision to start and continue a business is a complex choice governed by an individual's perception of alternative income possibilities, training and education, business risk and opportunity, potential or existing demand for the entrepreneur's product or service, role model influences and capital availability. Taken together, the model offered in this chapter, and the review of the literature in chapter 3 have emphasized all of these factors.

The model in this section predicts that increased payment for outside, alternative employment coupled with greater opportunities for black professionals and managers decrease the likelihood of formations of new black-owned firms and lower the chances of existing firms continuing. These relationships, however, are not simple. For marginal entrepreneurs, greater available pay in alternative, outside employment is always a potential lure unless they are committed entrepreneurial personalities with relatively high reservation or certainty equivalent wage requirements. For the most able and talented black entrepreneurs, the extent and nature of black professional and mangerial opportunities in their geographic area is probably the primary opportunity cost that is periodically reviewed. The literature review, in addition, concludes that for those who remain as entreprenuers, the performance of their firms should be positively related to their level of human capital. This inference is also quite clear from our model. In addition to education, however, the literature indicated that areas with high levels of black professional and managerial employment also reflect substantial availability of business knowledge as well as the influence of positive role models. Our model also suggests that those with large amounts of human capital have demonstrated a willingness to invest for future returns. Thus, larger number of individuals with greater amounts of human capital implies a greater likelihood of investing both time and resources into business development.

Formations and continuations of black-owned firms are projected in this model to be directly related to upswings in the business cycle, with failures and low start-ups directly associated with economic downturns. This operates both through the impact of business cycle activity on the derived demand function for entrepreneurship as a factor of production, and through its impact on changing perceptions of risk and uncertainty. Business cycle activity is also seen here as greatly influencing the ability of the entrepreneur to generate internal, investment funds for the support, continuance, and growth of the firm.

Factors in addition to business cycle activity which impact environmental risk and uncertainty are seen as significantly impacting both the employment size of the firm and number of entrepreneurs willing to start new ventures. Events and exogenous impacts which increase area-wide risk and uncertainty concurrently lower the reservation or certainty equivalent wage at which individuals choose outside employee status and, hence, decrease the number of start-ups and continuations. Such factors may include significant population shifts and population - outflight, changes in the level of the area's overall industrial development, and significant shifts in the tax base and personal income, among others.

The model also contends that persons with greater personal wealth including those with greater access to investment funds from relatively wealthy friends and family have a greater capacity to assume risk and start new ventures of larger size. This implies that areas with greater black median family income should be better equipped to generate greater savings and larger number of formations. This assocation also holds for the ability to sustain business continuations over longer periods of time since new ventures require periodic capital infusions especially during the early stages of operation.

The importance of such equity capital has been supported in the literature by Bearse[34] who found that family financial assets were strongly and positively related to the likelihood of individuals becoming entrepreneurs. Asian-Americans, for instance, were found to have both the highest level of family assets and the highest business formation rates among all minority groups. Blacks, on the other hand, had the lowest wealth holdings of any racial/ethnic group and the lowest rates of business formation.

Historically, low personal financial assets have driven black entrepreneurs, out of necessity, to seek financing from external sources. Our model also demonstrates, in part, that unwarranted discrimination acts as an effective capital tariff which greatly limits the ability of blacks to start and continue businesses. Discrimination can also act as a barrier by affecting costs of materials relative to preferred rates, access to information, and bonding requirements. The ability to start and maintain businesses under barriers which effectively raise cost curves add to the myriad of problems already besetting black businessmen. Historically, government loan programs specifically targeted to minority entrepreneurs have sought to help temper this problem of access to outside capital. However, the evidence on the sufficiency of these loan aid programs, the soundness of their design, and their actual impact is quite mixed. Recent work has indicated some significant impacts of SBA funding on the receipt growth of black-owned businesses in the non-South, but not on total black firm growth. An investigation of the impact of SBA funding on a disaggregated measure of changes in total black firms by failures and formations, therefore, seems warranted. The literature is also quite mixed concerning the role of external capital from black banks on black-owned businesses with more recent work, again, suggesting some modest, quite generalized impact. More specific impacts are not now clearly understood.

Chapter V

EMPIRICAL METHODOLOGY, PREDICTIONS, AND DATA

EMPIRICAL APPROACH

This section will outline the hypothesized relationships drawn from the theoretical model and review of the literature, and discuss the criterion and explanatory variables used to measure these relationships. In general, the theoretical model and the minority business literature suggest four or five inclusive factors impacting minority business development. These factors include risk and opportunity cost factors, the capital access factor, the market demand factor and the business human capital factor. Several specific variables can be listed under each of these factors and used to represent their respective factor's impact on minority business development. We will identify each of these variables under their respective factor group classification, and discuss their specific expected impacts. However, it is neither necessary nor desirable to include all such feasible variables in the actual estimating equation. To do so would cause unnecessary redundancy and multicollinearity among the estimators. It is largely for this reason that we have chosen to augment the multiple regression approach with the multivariate technique of factor analysis to refine the final estimation form. The second section of this chapter will, therefore, present the varimax orthogonal rotation factor solution which will aid in the selection of variables for the final estimation equation. The final estimating equation should be a fairly efficient model with minimal multicollinearity, but which, nonetheless, will be well specified and adequately represent the pertinent causal impacts.

The empirical model will investigate various measures of business change and development. These criterion measures include firm formations and number of business failures between 1972 and 1977 by both geographical location and industry classification. It is important to have black firm formations measured in per capita or per 1000 black population terms to correct for heteroscedasticity stemming from varying sizes among standard metropolitan statistical areas (SMSAs).[1] Furthermore, black firm formations should be measured in per capita terms, and not as a ratio of formations to total number of firms, since several SMSAs had no firms in existence in some industries in 1972, but had firms form in those industries over the interim period. Failure rates, on the other hand, are measured as the ratio of failed firms from 1972 - 1977 to the total number of black-owned firms in the initial period of 1972. Firm failures per capita would be inappropriate since greater number of firms per capita in the initial period would directly imply, by itself, greater number of failures per capita. This measure of firm failure rates also minimizes the possibility of heteroscedastic error terms. In addition, all formation and failure measures are segmented into firms with paid employees and by firms without employees to capture and differentiate between larger firms with employment effects and those which generate no employment. The dynamics of each set is sufficiently different to justify this procedure. Both descriptive data previously discussed regarding the relationship between firm size and failure rates, and preliminary OLS estimates by Handy and Swinton[2] (1984) indicate that this is indeed the case.

The empirical model reflects the summary causal factors identified in the literature and theoretical section. These factors include risk and opportunity cost variables (r), capital access variables (k), market demand variables (d), and business human captial variables (hc). The general functional forms are, therefore,

(i) $\quad G_{is}^{WE} = f(r_s, k_s, d_s, hc_s)$

   where G_{is}^{WE} = A measure of business development or failure type i in metropolitan area s = 1,. . .,155, for firms with paid employees.

(ii) $\quad G_{is}^{NE} = f(r_s, k_s, d_s, hc_s)$

   where G_{is}^{NE} = A measure of business development or failure type i in metropolitan area s= 1,. . .,155, for firms with no paid employees.

(iii) $\quad G_{is,j}^{WE} = f(r_s, k_s, d_s \, hc_s)$

   where, $G_{is,j}^{WE}$ = A measure of development or failure type i in s metropolitan areas for firms with paid employees over j=1,. . .,7 non-agricultural industries.

   and

(iv) $\quad G_{is,j}^{NE} = f(r_s, k_s, d_s, hc_s)$

   where, $G_{is,j}^{NE}$ = A measure of development or failure type i in s metropolitan areas for firms without paid employees over j=1,. . .,7 non-agricultural industries.

A discussion of the feasible variables which can reasonably be used to measure these respective causal factors follows.

Opportunity Cost Variables

The theoretical model explicitly predicts that factors which increase the opportunity cost of entrepreneurial employment relative to other career opportunities retards black business ownership. Variables employed to represent

125

this impact include the change in black professional and managerial employment in large corporations, changes in educational attainment, and changes in the rate of unemployment. The reasons for the selection of these variables are discussed below.

a. Black Professional and Managerial Opportunities

The relative number of black professionals and managers (PRMN) working for large corporations is related to a number of dimensions concerning the black-owned business sector. First, the opportunity costs involved in staying self-employed increase as the opportunities for black professionals and managers increase in the corporate sector (PRMNDIF). The high opportunity cost involved is reflected in two ways. First, there will be some entrepreneurs who will actively withdraw from self-employment as new opportunities for black professionals and managers increase in the corporate sector. Second, while greater employment opportunities for black professionals and managers may , itself, signal a favorable environment within which to start new ventures, nonparticipation in self-employment by those in the corporate sector who possess superior business human capital means that the black business sector, as a whole, has a lower level of human capital (managerial knowledge and professionalism) than otherwise-- which also negatively impacts black business continutations. A relatively higher percentage of black professionals and managers within an SMSA is, therefore, a two-edged sword. It may reflect a positive environment of relative greater opportunities for blacks, on one hand, but high opportunity costs of self-employment on the other. As a proxy for the stock of business human capital and business knowledge in the area we would expect a positive relationship with measures of black-owned business development, and an inverse relationship with firm failures. On the other hand, we

126

would expect the higher opportunity costs associated with increasing professional and management opportunities to be inversely associated with black firm formations and directly associated with black firm failures. Of the two measures, the change in professional and managerial opportunities (PRMNDIF) is postulated to be somewhat more desirable since it measures opportunity costs concurrent with decisions to start or leave self-employment over the time period under investigation.

b. Changes in Educational Attainment

Changes in educational attainment have two different possible impacts on black business development. First, greater levels of black adult education, representing the human capital dimension, should positively impact black firm formation and continuation. But secondly, it also reflects changes in opportunity costs of self-employment. A negative relation between higher educational attainment and self-employment measures would reflect a tendency of better educated persons not electing to go into business for themselves, but rather choosing to employ their greater general training in the larger outside, alternative employment world. A priori, it is difficult to decide whether changes in years of educational attainment within areas, or differences in years of educational attainment between areas is most appropriate to measure this impact. The factor analysis results, to be discussed later in the chapter, however, strongly suggest using changes in years of educational attainment over time to measure both changing opportunity costs and general training since levels of black educational attainment are highly collinear with black family income.

c. Changes in the Rate of Unemployment

In addition to measuring the impact of changes in business cycle activity on rates of firm failure, changes in the rate of unemployment may well also measure changes in perceived opportunity costs of starting a new business. The State of Small Business: Report of the President, the annual report of the Small Business Administration, for instance, conjectured that higher unemployment rates should increase minority small business formation since rising unemployment lowers the opportunity cost of self-employment. The SBA reasons that many unemployed persons feel that they forego nothing by starting their own business since fewer jobs are available during periods of economic decline. This, however, seems to be a very narrow interpretation of opportunity costs since significant declines in the business cycle may well also signal greater perceived risks to committing oneself to running a business since personal resources may be quite low during periods of economic decline. Overall, we hypothesize that the greater perceived risk to starting new ventures during periods of economic decline outweighs opportunity cost evaluations. We, therefore, hypothesize a significant inverse relationship between changes in unemployment rates and new black-owned business formations.

Variables Measuring Capital Access

In general, there are three channels of access to capital for small businesses: (i) loans or venture capital from a financial intermediary such as a bank or venture capitalist firm, (ii) personal savings and investment from family and friends, and/or (iii) loans or guarantees from government programs.

128

a. Loans from Black-owned Banks

The availability of capital to black-owned firms from financial intermediaries is proxied here by the amount of loans made available by black banks to such businesses, and the change in these funds over time. Ideally, some measure of availability of financing from non-black financial institutions to black-owned businesses would also be desirable, but no such data exists. There is, in addition, a large and venerable literature on black banking and its role in the black business community which can be further enhanced here. The literature is largely critical of the impact of black banks on business development because of its small size and conservative banking practices. However, as also indicated in the literature review, Boorman,[3] and Bates and Bradford[4] have conducted studies which indicate that newer black-owned banks should positively impact business development. Under our theoretical framework, we hypothesize a positive bank loan impact since banking institutions are more likely to screen applicants on the basis of their past performance and credit ratings then are government programs to businessmen. However, this hypothesized relationship should be qualified due to threshold effects whereby the size of the loans from black-owned banks might not be of sufficient magnitude to alter firm failures.

b. Savings from Black Median Family Income

Data on personal assets and funds from family and friends available to minority entrepreneurs by race and location is, of course, not available. It is a widely accepted view, however, that a high correlation exists between family income and the ability to generate savings for new small ventures. Differences in black median family income between metropolitan areas are, therefore, included to represent the ability to generate such personal funds. Higher median family income by geographical location is hypothesized to positively affect the ability of black entrepreneurs to start new ventures and maintain their firms.

c. Government Capital Assistance

The impact of government financing programs is hypothesized to be ambiguous since the availablity of such loans may both increase failures and formations by (i) simultaneously lowering the opportunity costs for both successful and failing entrepreneurs, and (ii) increasing the liability position of firms which may not be able to sustain a long-term debt position.

Some individuals who invest retained net income over and above self-remuneration for business continuance and growth, thereby increasing the net worth of the firm, may also have the opportunity to earn more income in alternative, outside employment than they can pay themselves, in the foreseeable future, from their own business. While their total returns from self-employment may exceed that of outside employment, relatively low personal earnings after reinvesting in the net worth of the firm may begin to discourage such individuals from continuing in business.

Government capital assistance programs are best tailored for such individuals since these programs provide an opportunity to fill a capital investment need, and mitigate the hardship of constantly receiving low self-payment in order to undertake capital accumulation. Government capital assistance may allow such entrepreneurs the opportunity to pay themselves at least an amount equal to outside opportunities, thereby prolonging self-employment careers. The drawback (trade-off) is that these programs, by filling a capital need and allowing for greater self-remuneration, also increase the likelihood of marginal entrepreneurs choosing and continuing in self-employment when they should not. That is, even though marginal entrepreneurs have total returns from self-employment below that of outside alternatives (where $R = V_{se} - V_{alt} < 0$), government funds may allow them the opportunity to pay themselves comparable to outside pay.

Therefore, government assistance programs such as SBA will positively impact minority business development by aiding those with positive entrepreneurial aptitude and skills, but who suffer from capital shortage problems. It may, on the other hand, also increase the number of business failures by increasing the number of those who should not, under our theory, be self-employed, but who now find capital easier to obtain. Therefore, its net impact on minority business development is ambiguous. The government aid measure is represented by total SBA loan programs since these are the most prevalent and comprehensive of government programs aiding black businesses. The impact of changes and fluctuations in SBA funding over time was selected over any single year loan amount since SBA money fluctuates within jurisdictions from year to year.

Market Demand Variables

a. Black Median Family Income and the Change in Black Population

Theoretical considerations, the literature, and common observation all indicate that greater markets and greater demand are a prerequisite to firm continuance and formation, and lower failure rates. Greater levels of potential demand in an area-- as represented by total per capita income in the SMSA -- are, therefore, hypothesized to have positive impact on receipt growth, formations and continuances. The level of demand for black-owned business products and services is primarily and most directly affected, of course, by the local black consumer market. Two variables represent different aspects of this market. First, black median family income (BFAMIN) reflects the income base for such products and services. Second, upon controlling for concentration of black population, the percentage growth in the black population itself (BLKPCH), ceteris paribus, should have a positive impact on measures of growth since it reflects a larger market in which to sell goods and services. The percentage change in the black population is projected here as representing "market widening," while changes in black median family income is projected to measure "market deepening." The level of black median family income is projected to measure the overall depth of the market.

b. Residential Segregation

The earlier literature emphasized the importance of protected segregated markets for black business products and services. With declining measures of segregated residential patterns during the 1970s (SEGDIF), some investigators hypothesized a dampening effect on the sales and growth of black businesses since they had to increasingly compete with business in general. Others, however, have stressed the growing availabilty of general markets to such businesses (SUINDIF) as an opportunity for expansion. The expected sign is, therefore, ambiguous here. Note, also that changes in the residential segregation measure (the Schnare index) differs from the SMSA-wide changes in black population concentration in that it measures the changes in the distribution of black population concentration across census tracts within the SMSA. We note that changes in residential segregation (SEGDIF) within SMSAs over the 1970's were modest compared to differences in residential segregation across metropolitan areas (SEG72) at any point in time.

132

The impact of residential segregation, therefore is better measured by differences in residential segregation across SMSAs in the initial period (SEG72).

Business Human Capital: Education and Level of Business Knowledge

The relative efficiency of black-owned general human capital is proxied by the educational attainment of the black adult population over 25 years of age by SMSA location. Theoretical considerations strongly suggest that both greater levels of education (BLKED70), and greater number of black professionals and managers per capita should positively impact growth. Higher levels of black professionals and managers per capita reflect a greater specific human capital base experience and knowledge from which to start and successfully maintain businesses, and a larger pool of those who have demonstrated a willingness to invest time and resources for future returns. The sign on changes in black professional and managerial opportunities (PRMNDIF) is ambiguous , however, since it also represents, under our theory, higher opportunity cost for self-employment.

It should be noted here that we use EEOC data on black professionals and managers[5] to serve as proxies for the total number of such black personnel in the SMSA. The assumption here is that relatively greater levels black professionals and managers reported by private industry to the EEOC, by metropolitan area, also reflect relatively greater levels of the total number of black professionals and managers by metropolitan area. This is largely confirmed by the very large correlation between the 1977 EEOC measure and the 1980 census measure of total black professionals and managers by SMSA (p = .96).[6] The problem, however, with using the decennial census data to directly measure this variable is two-fold. First, decennial census data does not reflect intervening years, as does the EEOC data;

133

and second, and more importantly, the Census Bureau changed the definition of professionals and managers between the 1970 and 1980 Censuses -- making comparison between the two censuses difficult.

Summary Measures of State-of-Nature Risk Between Standard Metropolitan Statistical Areas

Ideally, we would like to measure differences in risk and uncertainty between SMSAs in forming and continuing black small businesses by some measure of variance in performance among areas. However, this is not possible since ordinary least square estimates are based on analysis of variance. The dependent variable, failure rates, for instance, essentially measures variation in failure rates; thus a measure of risk based on variances in outcomes of failure or continuation rates (which is simply one minus the failure rate) as an explanatory variable would be inappropriate. We have, therefore, utilized various macro measures which summarize numerous characteristics which, in some general way, impact expectations and degree of uncertainty. While these are, admittedly, rough measures, we feel that by so interpreting (i) fluctuations in business cycle activity, (ii) initial differences in probability of self-employment between areas, and (iii) changes in concentration of black population, reflecting changing economic climate relative to possible white population outflight, we can add some further realism and richness to the analysis.

a. Business Cycle Activity

A number of investigators (e.g. Brimmer and Terrell; Bates; Handy and Swinton) contend that local unemployment rates should be inversely related to firm continuations and new firm formations, and directly related to number of failing firms. Both higher starting levels of unemployment across SMSAs (UNEMP72) and increases in unemployment rates (UNEMDIF) within SMSAs reflect a downturn in

134

local business activity which is associated with greater area-wide risk in starting and continuting firms. Of the two measures, however, changes in the rate of unemployment (UNEMDIF) is preferable since it directly measures business cycle activity.

b. Concentration of Black Population

While per capita income between 1972 and 1977 increased by $1730 in the 155 SMSAs covered by this study, and black median family income increased on average by $6760 between the 1970 and 1980 censuses in these same SMSAs, increasing concentrations of black population across metropolitan areas had a nonincreasing, slightly negative association with per capita income ($p= -0.067$) and a nonincreasing, slightly negative association with black median family income ($p= -0.064$). Consequently, increased black population concentration (PBLKDIF) was not associated with higher growth areas. This variable, however, does not appear to be as strong a candidate for reflecting declining economic areas, and therefore greater state-of-nature risk, as do downturns in business activity.

c. Probability of Self-Employment

If self-employed persons made the decision to become self-employed solely due to innate personal risk aversion, in the absense of any other influence on risk perceptions, then we would not expect any systematic differences in the probability of self-employment between SMSAs since it is reasonable to assume, ceteris paribus, that risk loving, risk neutral and risk averse persons would be similarly distributed across geographical areas. There would be no reason to expect more risk lovers or more risk averters per unit of population in any geographical area except for external environmental factors (e.g., gambling in

135

Reno or Las Vegas; or risk averse entrepreneurs capturing positive spillovers by locating in successful, high tech areas like Silicon Valley, California, or Triangle Park, North Carolina, or Route 128, Massachusetts). We therefore assume that significant differences in the probability of self-employment between SMSAs are largely a function of area differences in the state-of-nature which result in differences in actual and perceived risk and uncertainty in the area. The theoretical model also supports this reasoning since greater risk and uncertainty was shown as resulting in individuals choosing market employment over entrepreneurial pursuits at lower certainty equivalent wages. Thus, all factors collectively impacting the degree of risk and uncertainty across areas simultaneously impact the percent of those in the population choosing self-employment across those areas.

Differentials in the probability of self-employment by geographical area, as discussed above, reflect differentials in area conditions. Areas experiencing higher probability of self-employment must reflect, therefore, lower perceived area-wide, state-of-nature risks associated with being self-employed compared to areas with significantly lower self-employment per unit of population. Consequently, we expect a significant positive relationship between initial probability of self-employment (SELFEM), reflecting initial risk conditions in an area, and the number of firm formations over time in that area. We would also expect an inverse relationship between probability of initial levels of self-employment and number of failures over time per unit of population.

Since the probability of an event is the ratio of the number of times an event actually occurs divided by the total number of ways that event can possibly occur, the probability of self-employment within an SMSA is estimated by the ratio of black self-employed persons over the total black labor force (SELFEM).

Summary of Hypothesized Impacts on Black Business Development

	Formations	Failures
Risk & Opportunity Costs		
Change in Unemployment	−	+
Probability of Self-Employment	+	−
Percent Black Professionals & Managers	−	+
Increasing Black Population Concentration	−	+
Capital Access		
Increasing SBA loans	?	?
Initial level of SBA funds	?	?
Increasing Black Commercial Bank Loans	+	−
Level of Black Commercial Bank loans	+	−
Black Median Family Income	+	−
Market Demand		
Black Median Family Income	+	−
Total Per Capita Income	+	−
Percent Change in Black Population	+	−
Residential Segregation	?	?
Business Human Capital		
Years of Educational Attainment	+	−
Pool of Black Professionals and Managers	+	−

THE FINAL ESTIMATING EQUATION: SELECTING SURROGATE VARIABLES FOR THE REGRESSION ANALYSIS

Given the rather large number of explanatory variables which are eligible to represent various causal impacts, it becomes important to identify a limited number of appropriate variables for subsequent inclusion into the final estimating regression equation. Our a priori discussion of expected impacts of these variables has been helpful in identifying what we feel are the critical variables for inclusion in the final estimating equation. That discussion also outlined whether the intial value or change in the respective variables would be most appropriate. While

137

empirical investigations should ideally be largely guided by theoretical relationships, often a high degree of multicollinearity poses an efficiency problem in the estimators. Certainly, a researcher should not drop any variable with important theoretical impacts merely due to interdependency unless there is a clear understanding of how other related variables take account of this impact. Relatedly, however, specifications which can both minimize the multicollinearity problem and still adequately represent the important theoretical impacts are most desirable. A technique which can, therefore, aid in minimizing the efficiency problem and which can also aid in confirming or supporting the underlying theoretical dimensions of the model would prove quite useful.

Two related techniques were employed to assist in obtaining these desirable properties. The first approach involved deriving principle component estimates of regression coefficients for each variable. Such an approach would be very useful since it results in regression coefficients of orthogonally rotated variables which are independent of one another. Unfortunately, however, the results obtained from this technique were unstable because of the nonlinear specification of the black bank loan variable.[7] Principal component regression estimates require a strict linear relationship among explanatory and dependent variables, which does not hold in this model.

The second approach involves selecting variables from orthogonal factors in such a way as to minimize interdependency among the selected variables. This is known as the surrogate variable selection technique, and is discussed most notably in Hair, Tatham, and Grablowsky[8]; Press[9]; and Rummel.[10] Since we want to reduce the large number of eligible variables into a smaller set of largely uncorrelated, independent variables for subsequent use, an orthogonal rotation of

138

these variables by factor grouping is the preferred starting approach because the factors can be extracted in such a way that each factor is independent of all other factors.[11] By additionally specifying a varimax orthogonal rotation, we simplify the columns of the factor matrix which is equivalent to maximizing the variance of the squared loadings of every variable in each factor column. Each variable's factor loading expresses the correlation between that variable and the respective factor, with the squared factor loading indicating what percent of variance of the variable is explained by that factor. Consequently, variables loading most heavily on one given orthogonal factor, to which that variable is highly correlated and which explains a large percent of the variance in that variable, must by definition be largely uncorrelated with other variables whose variance is largely explained by other unrelated factors. Therefore, if two or more variables are highly correlated with one another, they would load on the same factor or factors:

> ...variables that are fairly strongly related will end up loading highly on the same factor(s).[12]

(The converse, however, is not true. Two or more variables loading on the same factor may or may not be highly correlated since they may each be correlated with an unobserved, underlying factor or other highly loading variables on that factor).

Thus, by selecting the variable with the highest loading on each respective varimax, orthogonally rotated factor, so that none of the selected variables load up heavily on the same factor, we can generate a set of variables with minimal multicollinearity. Moreover, by examining the varimax, orthogonal matrix and selecting the variable with the highest factor loading on each factor, we also generate a set of variables which can act as surrogates for each particular factor dimension:

If the researcher wants to reduce the larger number of variables into a smaller set of uncorrelated variables for subsequent use in a regression analysis, or other predictive techniques, then the orthogonal solution is the best.... Surrogate variables would be selected only when the factor rotation is orthogonal. This is because when the analyst is interested in using surrogate variables in subsequent analyses, he would like to observe to the extent possible the assumption of that the independent variables should be uncorrelated with each other. If the objective is to identify appropriate variables for subsequent application to other statistical techniques, then the researcher would examine the factor matrix and select the variable with the highest factor loading as a surrogate representative for a particular factor dimension.[13]

The uppermost objective of securing both an efficient and well specified model would be highly credible if the variables generated from the factor analysis closely matched the variables selected in our a priori discussion. It should be mentioned, however, that in applied work these two approaches do not, necessarily, provide two completely independent procedures for the selection of variables. Often theoretical considerations are critical in choosing variables from factors since several variables may load heavily and closely on the same factor. When this, in fact, occurred in several of our factors, we chose those variables which both loaded heavily and which either on a priori, theoretical grounds best represented the dimension being identified or which represented a more meaningful phenomenon from a policy standpoint.

Of the twenty seven factors generated, ten factors having eigenvalues greater than one were selected by the SPSS program for the final varimax rotated factor matrix. These ten factors collectively account for 72 percent of the variance of all twenty seven factors. From the factor analysis these ten factors selected under the latent root criterion,[14] in turn, collectively account for 83 percent of the variance or communality of formations of black-owned firms with paid employees across metropolitan areas, and 87 percent of the variance in formations of black firms with no paid employees. In addition, these ten factors, comprising the rotated factor matrix, account for only 40 percent of the variance in failures for black firms with paid employees, and 37 percent of the variance in failures of black firms with no paid employees. The initial feasible variable selections discussed earlier, therefore, appear to be quite good in explaining failure and formation of black-owned firms across standard metropolitan statistical areas.

The selection procedure for each variable used in the final estimating equation can be described as follows: Given the varimax rotated factor matrix show below, we go <u>across the row of each variable</u> and select the highest factor loading for that variable. These highest loadings are shown as the boxed-in numbers for each variable row. By going down the columns, however, we note that most factors have two or more explanatory variables with loadings that are significant and fairly close to one another. Two of the factors have direct, straightforward interpretations with one dominate explanatory variable loading. By utilizing the discussion of expected impacts and the structure of theoretical relationships, along with prior information on the extent of correlation between the variables, we are able to select variables which minimize multicollinearity and which collectively offer a specification which reflects the pertinent, underlying impacts. In what follows, we ignore the signs of the factor loadings since we are interested primarily in the magnitude of the regression weights and correlation coefficients represented by the orthogonal factor loadings.

TABLE 5.1

VARIMAX ROTATED FACTOR MATRIX

	FACTOR 1	FACTOR 2	FACTOR 3	FACTOR 4	FACTOR 5	FACTOR 6	FACTOR 7	FACTOR 8	FACTOR 9	FACTOR 10
PRMNDIF	0.17547	0.03906	0.16725	-0.14807	0.04548	0.10818	-0.04377	-0.24192	-0.19728	-0.09469
BBLNDIF	-0.10392	0.10077	0.06608	0.02840	0.09862	0.85184	0.05244	-0.03916	-0.11328	-0.14820
BBLNSQ	-0.03982	-0.50486	0.01401	-0.01909	0.00373	0.89080	-0.08890	-0.07235	-0.02265	0.02894
SBADIF	-0.08449	0.08822	-0.04232	-0.05386	0.03524	0.01813	0.07295	0.18136	-0.08580	0.21797
SELFEW7O	-0.05140	0.01659	0.05567	0.10412	0.23096	0.14202	0.47041	0.10764	0.28400	0.02372
SELFEWHDF	0.13182	0.17852	0.05361	0.12163	-0.02282	0.11578	0.06533	-0.03640	0.16713	0.06443
SBANE	-0.14981	0.18569	0.14548	-0.04050	0.13942	-0.00971	-0.11342	0.86130	0.01918	-0.04362
SBANC	-0.03389	0.08911	-0.04403	0.02841	-0.00423	0.12834	-0.04185	0.06575	-0.03860	0.04807
SBASO	-0.09830	0.17419	0.00932	-0.01123	0.08947	0.14138	-0.09776	0.00572	0.04914	0.09041
BLKPCH	-0.00972	0.05314	-0.04108	-0.77833	0.28607	0.05457	0.11356	-0.06231	0.03842	0.14028
UNEWDIF	-0.34874	-0.15059	0.33218	0.09230	0.10842	0.20195	-0.12088	0.12693	0.16380	0.04715
PBLKDIF	0.19821	-0.18059	0.41802	-0.08941	0.15697	0.05717	0.11600	-0.07145	0.27438	0.13325
SUINDIF	-0.01341	0.05077	0.07755	-0.09954	0.00445	0.21167	-0.14363	0.13193	0.26085	0.23748
SEGDIF	0.13183	-0.00367	0.00889	0.04560	0.38212	0.04980	-0.03898	-0.04070	-0.03729	0.01528
BFINDIF	-0.05881	-0.08673	0.05951	-0.00464	-0.04081	0.01915	-0.05544	0.01345	0.15861	0.13886
SEG2	-0.14021	0.00407	0.16121	-0.06784	0.09806	0.10038	-0.15083	0.10695	0.18643	-0.13886
PERBLK2	0.79563	0.02198	0.14185	0.11763	-0.13847	-0.08904	0.04630	0.34845	0.12216	0.11037
PRMN72	0.67248	0.06880	0.06880	0.11439	-0.24807	0.08204	0.08586	0.05828	0.08694	0.39307
BLKEO7O	0.34765	0.01831	0.16895	0.17059	0.14717	0.01833	0.03621	0.05828	0.15359	-0.08009
BLK7DJF	0.81369	0.00172	0.30561	0.57643	-0.05686	0.06984	0.30538	0.07208	0.05369	-0.03780
BFAMIN2	0.28155	0.10974	0.04276	0.11855	0.20488	0.05152	0.02303	0.53442	-0.02818	0.11287
NEIN72	0.44034	-0.02289	0.15661	0.28800	0.09978	0.07940	0.34355	0.84022	-0.05068	0.05248
NCIN72	-0.71571	-0.02289	0.00280	0.07194	-0.11982	-0.02289	0.18484	0.15465	-0.02818	0.04898
SOIN72	0.84846	0.57729	0.05044	0.31810	0.12881	0.16686	-0.02397	0.08887	0.13490	0.32740
SBA72	0.30171	0.18449	0.16950	0.08488	0.38347	-0.08968	-0.04453	0.10944	0.16512	0.04898
BLN72	0.76427	-0.03788				-0.07332	-0.07209	0.13461	0.13080	0.11239
SURINC2										

Variables loading on factor 2 and factor 6, respectively, indicate straightforward variable selections. Factor 2 clearly represents the impact of SBA loans. The loading of the change in SBA loans (SBADIF) of the excluded Western regional dummy (which is the comparison base) is .90, with the differential impact of SBA loans in the Midwest (SBANC) also loading at .90 . The next highest loading is SBA loans in the single, initial year of 1972 (SBA72). Of two measures, the movement of SBA loans by metropolitan areas over the 1972-1977 period is the preferable measure. The first time-point is measured as the average of 1971 and 1972 loans, with the end point represented by the average of 1976 and 1977 loans. The movement of SBA loans to black businessman, therefore, takes account of four years of SBA performance, rather than just a single year. Factor 6 clearly represents the nonlinear impact of changes in loans from black-owned banks (BBLNDIF), with a loading of over .85.

Factor 1 shows five highly correlated variables loading significantly. These include black median family income (BFAMIN2), years of educational attainment for blacks (BLKED70), the concentration of black population (PERBLK2), total per capita income (SURINC2), and the initial level of black professional and managerial employment (PRMN72). We should, of course, expect levels of black median family income to be highly correlated with median years of black educational attainment, with black professional and managerial opportunities, and with total per capita income of the area, and for all of them to load highly on the same factor. We chose black median family income as the most important variable from this factor since it represents both the basis of savings in the black community and market demand for black firms' goods and services. The concentration of black population in the intial year is highly correlated with residential segregation, and highly negatively correlated with black family income, years of black educational

143

attainment, and black professional and management opportunities. Its inclusion in the final equation, therefore, would greatly increase the risk of multicollinearity, while at the same time it can be largely proxied by residential segregation across metropolitan areas. Per capita income in the area is less specific in its impact on black business than black median income; moreover the correlation between total per capita and black median family income is so high that both need not be included. The initial level of black professional and managerial opportunities was postulated to be less important than changes in black professional and managerial opportunities as a reflection of changing opportunity costs. Lastly, years of black adult educational attainment in the initial period and black family income are so highly correlated that multicollinearity would certainly be a problem if both were included. Moreover, changes in educational attainment for black adults over 25 would better reflect changes in human capital and concomitant opportunity costs.

Just as initial levels of black median family income, professional and managerial opportunities, and total per capita income were highly correlated and loading on the same factor, so too are the changes in these three variables highly correlated and loading on the same factor--factor 3. Levels of Black median family income are already represented, while changes in total per capita income (SUINDIF) were judged to be less specific than black income measures. On the hand, based on our theoretical model, changes in black professional and managerial opportunities (PRMNDIF) in each area should be selected because of its great importance in representing changing opportunity costs in the area.

Factor 4 has the percent change in the black population (BLKPCH), representing the extent of market widening for black firms' goods and services, and changes in residential segregation (SEGDIF) loading most heavily. The percent change in the black population was selected from this factor to represent the market widening impact rather than the change in residential segregation. The change in residential segregation is small compared to differences in the levels of residential segregation between cities.

Factor 5, however, has such differences in levels of residential segregation (SEG2) loading heavily, along with changes in years of black educational attainment for the black adult population (BLKEDIF). In this one case we selected both variables for inclusion in the final estimating equation. Clearly, large differences in levels of residential segregation between cities are more important than comparatively minor changes in residential segregation within cities. This is reflected in the fact that the ranking of cities by residential segregation is largely unchanged between 1970 and 1980. Moreover, it is important to account for changes in the human capital impact of education especially since the very high correlation between levels of education and levels of median family income resulted in levels of education being waived and proxied by the income measure.

Using both changes in years of adult education and differences in levels of residential segregation, additionally, poses no problem in multicollinearity even though they both load on the same factor. Again, we should be reminded that while highly correlated variables will load on the same factor, the converse does not hold that all variables loading highly on the same factor are highly correlated. The correlation between the two variables is a modest .20. Consistently, the regression results for formations of firms with paid employees and for firms without employees, to be discussed in the next chapter, both indicate that no interdependency problem exists between these two variables. Both changes in educational attainment, and levels of residential segregation are significant at the

.01 level in the equation for formations with paid employees , indicating no efficiency problem due to the presence of these variables. Likewise, segregation is significant in the equation for formation of firms without employees, while changes in education are not significant; but when segregation levels are dropped, changes in educational attainment still does not become significant, nor does its coefficient change to any degree. This again indicates no interdependency problem between the two variables.

Factor 7 has the percent of blacks self-employed in the initial period (SELFEM70) loading heavily along with changes in black population concentration (PBLKDIF). We have already alluded several times to the theoretical importance of the probability of self-employment in the initial period as a measure or indicator of area-wide risk. The changes in black to white or black to total population concentrations do not represent the widening of the market as well as the percent change in black population, nor was it judged to be a powerful predictor of risk and uncertainty in declining economic areas.

Both initial levels of bank loans (BLN72) and change in the percent of blacks self-employed (SELFEMDF) load significantly on factor 9. While the change in percent self-employed is by far the largest loading on that factor it matches too closely the nature of the phenomena we are trying to explain since the small firm and the self-employed entrepreneur are virtually synonymous. Changes in one directly reflect changes in the other . This correspondence, however, should not be confused with the percent of blacks self-employed in the initial, starting period, which was previously selected. The number of those already in business does not, by itself, guarantee either higher or lower failure rates, or greater or fewer new firms forming over ensuing periods of time. The selection of initial levels of black bank loans (BLN72) from this factor completes the picture regarding as important capital access variable with important policy implications.

Lastly, changes in unemployment rates (UNEMDIF) load significantly on factor 10, along with SBA loans in the South (SBASO), changes in years of black education, and initial black bank loans. Changes in education, and levels of black bank loans are already represented, as is SBA activity. From the correlation matrix, we observe also that changes in unemployment are not particularly associated with these variables. Nonetheless, changes in unemployment rates are a critical measure of the state-of nature impact reflected in business cycle activity, and should be utilized in the estimating equation.

By considering jointly both the loadings of all eligible variables in the rotated factor matrix and the nature of interdependency among all the eligible variables, along with the theoretical model and discussion of expected impacts, we have generated a consistent, reasonable set of variables for the final estimating equation. The final equation has no two variables having more than a .28 bivariate correlation, and all the major projected underlying causal factors are represented. The final estimation equation, therefore, appears as follows,

$$
\begin{aligned}
G = \ & B_0 + B_1 \text{ BFAMIN*REGION} + B_2 \text{ PRMNDIF} + B_3 \text{ SELFEM72} \\
& + B_4 \text{ SBA*REGION} + B_5 \text{ BLKPCH} + B_6 \text{ BBLNDIF} + B_7 \text{ BBLNSQ} \\
& + B_8 \text{ BLKEDIF} + B_9 \text{ SEG72} + B_{10} \text{ BLN72} + B_{11} \text{ UNEMDIF} + e
\end{aligned}
$$

DATA CONSTRAINTS AND PREVIOUS WORK

Systematic data collection concerning black and other minority-owned businesses began only as recently as 1969. Limitations in previous research to a large extent reflect the limited data available until recently. A review of the literature suggests that, on the whole, previous studies have been circumscribed by some combination of five limitations. These limitations include, (1) overdependence on voluntary, self-reported questionnaire data, (2) nonrecognition of inherent response and selection bias in the type and number of firms analyzed, (3) restriction to single year cross sectional data, (4) the exclusive use of internal factors of the firm with no allowance for larger economic forces, and (5) little or no explicit methodology to investigate factors of change and growth in minority business enterprise in its entirety.

Minority business research initially relied quite heavily on firm loan data from the Small Business Administration (SBA) to generate their sample of firms.[15] The majority of these loans were funded under the SBA's Economic Opportunity Loan programs (EOL) targeting assistance ot the disadvantaged. Beginning in 1965, EOL programs sought to assist solely those entrepreneurs who were living in poverty. Later, program eligibility required loan applicants to be economically and socially disadvantaged. While the high incidence of loan defaults observed in virtually every study utilizing the EOL data base was, in fact, consistent with the programs' underlying philosophy of targeting assistance, research results were heavily biased. Investigations based on that data source were assured of finding high incidences of defaults and marginal businesses enterprises. In addition, the early studies based upon non-governmental data sources were similarly skewed because the sample selection also guaranteed an over-representation of weaker firms.[16]

At the other end of the spectrum, more recent micro studies drawn from Dun and Bradstreet files overrepresent the best, most credit-worthy minority firms.[17] Several of these studies found that upon controlling for size, minority businesses were equal to, and often performed better than similarly sized majority firms by all measures of profitability. Studies utilizing either of these data sources do contain very useful information once it is understood just what class of firms are being investigated. A micro data base would be quite useful in drawing conclusions about the overall nature of minority-owned business if it were truely a random sample of firms. The micro sets used thus far, however, are really stratified samples. When we compare, for instance, the size of the sampled Dun and Bradstreet firms to SBA assisted firms this difference clearly emerges. Upon comparing Dun and Bradstreet with SBA firms in the non-traditional areas of wholesale trade, manufacturing, and construction, it is clear that Dun and Bradstreet minority firms are three to five times larger than their SBA counterparts (see Table 5.2).

TABLE 5.2
Comparisons of Minority Business Size
SBA Loan Data Versus D&B Sample of Firms
1975–1978

A. Median Employees Per Firm:

	I	II	III
			SBA Employment/ D&B Employment
	SBA	D&B	(I/II)
Wholesale	2.3 - 2.7	10.6	21.7 - 25.5%
Construction	4.3 - 4.7	11.7	36.7 - 40.2%
Manufacturing	5.0 - 6.8	25.0	20.0 - 27.2%

B. Mean Employees Per Firms:

	I	II	III
			SBA Employment/ D&B Employment
	SBA	D&B	(I/II)
Wholesale	5.8	20.0	29.0%
Construction	7.7	23.7	32.5%
Manufacturing	21.5	59.2	21.1%

SOURCE: Bates, Furino, and Wadsworth (1983, p. 111).

Studies which restrict their investigation to Dun and Bradstreet sampled minority-owned firms, therefore, do not have a random sample of minority-owned firms since D&B, in effect, truncates the smaller firms from their sample. As a result, such studies do not take account of the strong and consistent relationship between firm size and expected failure rate.[18] When investigating failure and formation rates there is, therefore, the additional requirement of either (i) comparing smaller firms with no employees to larger firms with paid employees, or (ii) accounting for firm size as an explicit explanatory variable. Consequently, studies which take as observations only SBA assisted firms or D&B sampled firms suffer from selectivity bias.

The sources used for measuring the dependent and explanatory variables in our model come from a variety of public sources. Much of the data, however, was either unpublished or not available to the general public, and required special tabulations and clearance for use in the study. A short listing of references by variable designation is given below.

Dependent Variables:

(1)   Black-Owned Firm Formations and Failures between 1972 and 1977 by Industry: Compiled from special tabulations by the U.S. Bureau of the Census. The Enterprise Statistics Division of the Census derived a file of Matched and Unmatched Minority-Owned Business Records 1972/1977 by Standard Metropolitan Statistical Area from micro files permitting identification of employers from either IRS identification numbers or social security numbers in both 1972 and 1977. If the firm was on the 1977 file, but not on the 1972 file, it was counted as a formation. If found on the 1972 file, but not on the 1977 file it was counted as a failure. Firms found in both files were counted as continuations or survivors over that five year period. Within each SMSA there are also records for the major industry divisions by one digit SIC classification. The data is available in four volumes with clearance from the Research Division of the Minority Business Development Agency, U.S. Department of Commerce.

Explanatory Variables:

(1)   Black Professionals and Managers 1972, 1977 Hired by Corporations: Compiled from the 1973 and 1978 EEOC Report, Minorities and Women in Private Industry, Vols. 1 and 2 (U.S., Equal Employment Opportunity Commission, Washington, D.C.)

(2)   Black Bank Loans: Derived from 1971, 1972 and 1976, 1977 data compiled by the Federal Reserve Bank of Atlanta, and by the U.S. Federal Reserve Bank, Washington, D.C. from the Consolidated Report of Condition for A Bank and Its Domestic and Foreign Subsidiaries, various years.

(3)   Small Business Administration Loan Assistance Programs: Derived from compilation done by special computer runs across 3,000 counties nationwide for the years 1971, 1972, 1976 and 1977, (U.S. Small Business Administration, Washington, D.C., Reports Management Division, Summary Listing of Approved Business Loans to Blacks in the Years 1971, 1972, 1976 and 1977).

(4)   Unemployment Rate by SMSA, 1977 and 1972: State and Metropolitan Area Data Book, 1979 (Bureau of the Census); and Ibid, 1977 .

(5) Total Black Population by SMSA, 1972: Intrepolated from 1970 Current Population Reports, series P-25, Nos. 814-863 (U.S. Bureau of the Census).

Total Black Population by SMSA, 1977: Interpolated from Census of Population, 1980, Standard Metropolitan Statistical Areas and Standard Consolidated Statistical Areas (U.S. Bureau of the Census).

(6) Total Income Per Capita by SMSA, 1972: Interpolated from County and City Data Book, 1977, Table 3, Items 33-48, (U.S. Bureau of the Census).

Total Income Per Capita by SMSA, 1977: Interpolated from State and Metropolitan Area Data Book, 1979, Table B, Items 233-248, (U.S. Bureau of the Census).

(7) Segregation Index, 1972: Taken from Ann Schnare, Residential Segregation by Race in U.S. Metropolitan Areas (Washington, D.C., Urban Institute, 1977).

Segregation Index, 1977: Schnare Index calculated by author from the STF-1A Tape File on population counts by race for all census tracts from the U.S. 1980 Census. The counts were extracted from 34,000 census tracts by the Social and Behavioral Sciences Lab at the University of South Carolina.

(8) Black Median Family Income, 1972: Interpolated from the General Social and Economic Characteristics of Standard Metropolitan Statistical Areas, 1970 (U.S. Bureau of the Census).

Black Median Family Income, 1977: Interpolated from the STF-3C Summary Tape on the 1980 Social, Economic and Housing Characteristics by Standard Metropolitan Statistical Areas by the University of Georgia, Office of Computing and Information Services.

(9) Black Years of Education (Persons 25 years of age and over), 1972: General Social and Economic Characteristics of Standard Metropolitan Statistical Areas, 1970, Table 183 (U.S. Bureau of the Census).

Black Years of Education (Persons 25 years of age and over) 1977: Proxied by data from the STF-3C Summary Tape on the 198 Social, Economic and Housing Characteristics by SMSA's (University of Georgia, Office of Computing and Information Services).

(10) Number of Blacks Self-Employed by SMSA, 1972: Derived from the Detailed Characteristics, 1970 Census of Population. PC (1), by State within which each SMSA is located. Table 186, "Industry of Employed Persons by Class of Worker, Race and Sex," from each state volume.

Number of Blacks Self-Employed by SMSA, 1977: Derived from the Detailed Population Characteristics, 1980 Census of Population, PC80 - 1 -D, by State within which SMSA is located. Table 229 of each state volume, "Industry of Employed Persons by Class of Worker, Hours Worked, Sex, Race, and Spanish Origin."

Chapter VI

RESULTS

In this chapter we employ the final estimating equation developed in chapter five to examine formations and failure rates of black-owned firms across metropolitan areas. Both formations per 1000 black population for firms with and without employees, and firm failures as a percentage of total firms, with and without paid employees, were analyzed. In addition, it was judged that further useful information could be acquired by looking at failures and formations of firms by one digit industry classification. Consequently, impacts on failures and formations of black-owned firms in (i) construction, (ii) manufacturing, (iii) transportation, (iv) wholesale trade, (v) retail trade, (vi) services and (vii) finance, insurance, and real estate for each employee classification were also examined.

In general, the results indicate that area-wide conditions are much better at explaining firm formations than firm failures. Across all industries, the equation for the formation of small firms without paid employees had a coefficient of determination (R^2) equal to .75, with a highly significant F statistic of 21.3. Formation of small retail, services, and finance, insurance and real estate firms without paid employees also had significant fits, with 62 percent, 75 percent and 72 percent of their variances, respectively, being explained. Among the other remaining industries, the equations for formations of small firms with no employees were also significant with 32 percent to 50 percent of the observed

153

variation accounted for by the model. (See Table 6.1). Among larger black-owned firms with paid employees, the formation regression equation accounted for 70 percent of variance in the services industry. Across all other industries, formations of larger firms with paid employees had 20 to 46 percent of their variance accounted for by the regression model. (See Table 6.2).

Aggregated across all industries, the model explained only 23 percent of the variation in failures for small firms with no employees, and 22 percent of the variance in failures for larger firms with paid employees. (See Table 6.3). The model also behaved somewhat differently for failures than for formations. Unlike the formation regression, which was quite straightforward, we employed the Box-Cox procedure to choose the appropriate functional form for predicting failure rates.[1] Results from this procedure indicated that the semi-log form provided the best fit for the failure rate of small firms with no employees, and for firms with paid employees aggregated across all industries. Moreover, with the exception of the retail sector, the model was wholly unsuccessful in explaining failure rates of black-owned firms by specific industries. The F statistic for failure rates in every industry, across all employment categories, except for retailing, was less than the critical value. Differences in macro conditions do not appear, therefore, to be very helpful in explaining failure rates. Upon reflection, however, this is not surprising considering the small range of variation in black firm failure rates, shown in table 2.6, both among industries within SMSAs and within industries among SMSAs. In contrast, both the range of formation rates among industries and the coefficient of variation of formations within any industry, across SMSAs, are much larger than that of failure rates. As such, the variance to be explained for formations is greater than the variance to be explained for failures -- resulting in a much better fit for formations compared to failures.

DEFINITION OF VARIABLES

The respective impacts of the explanatory variables on black firm formation and black firm failure across employment categories are shown in Tables 6.1, 6.2, and 6.3. These variables are all defined across standard metropolitan statistical areas as follows:

BLKEDIF = change in years of black educational attainment over the 1970's.

PRMNDIF = change in number of black managers and professionals working in large corporations between 1972 and 1977.

SELEM72 = number of blacks self-employed in the initial period, 1972.

BBLNDIF = change in loans generated from black-owned commercial banks over the 1972-1977 period.

BBLNSQ = the square of black-owned commercial bank loans (corrects for heteroscedasticity associated with this variable).

BLN72 = amount of black commercial bank loans in the initial period, 1971-1972.

SBAWEST = change in total SBA loans in the western region of the United States over the 1972-1977 period.

SBANE = change in total SBA loans in the eastern region of the United States over the 1972-1977. period.

SBANC = change in total SBA loans in the central region on the United States over the 1972-1977 period.

SBASO = change in total SBA loans in the southern region of the United States over the 1972-1977 period.

BLKCH = percentage change in black population over 1972-1977 period.

WSTBFAMIN = black median family income in the western region of the United States in the initial period.

NEBFAMIN = black median family income in the northeastern region of the United States in the initial period.

NCBFAMIN = black median family income in the northcentral region of the United States.

SOBFAMIN = black median family income in the southern region of the United States.

SEGRE72 = residential segregation index in the initial period.

UNEMDIF = change in unemployment rates over the 1972-1977 period.

155

In what follows, we examine each of the respective causal impacts on formations and failures. In discussing each variable, we integrate findings regarding specific industry effects, when possible, to give a more complete picture of that variable's influence on firm formation and performance.

CHANGES IN BLACK ADULT EDUCATIONAL ATTAINMENT

The results suggest that metropolitan areas experiencing increasing levels of black educational attainment over the 1970's were inversely associated with the formation of new black-owned businesses. Increasing levels of black educational attainment were significantly associated with lower levels of new business formations in small retail establishments, small construction firms with no paid employees, and small manufacturing firms with no employees. (See Table 6.1) In other words, places with improving educational attainment were less likely to form black-owned sole proprietorships and small partnerships in retail, construction, and manufacturing. On the other hand, small wholesale establishments were more likely to form in areas with rising educational attainment. The story is similar for the establishment of larger new firms with paid employees. Increasing levels of black adult education were associated with lower formation of larger firms in the services and retail sectors, as well as in transportation. Overall, rising levels of education were associated with lower formations of larger black-owned businesses, with paid employees, across all industries taken as a whole (Table 6.2).

This suggests that the opportunity costs of becoming self-employed in SMSAs where persons are experiencing increasing levels of education are high. This result, however, should be interpreted with some caution since, first, higher _initial_ levels of black adult education at any point in time, across SMSAs, are highly correlated with black-owned firm formations, as shown in the bivariate correlation matrix.

156

Second, when income is dropped from the equation and initial levels of education among SMSAs are introduced in its place, there is a direct association between firm formations and levels of education.

Increasing levels of educational attainment over time, within SMSAs, were not associated with failure rates either across black firms with paid employees, or for black firms with no employees. Moreover, when initial levels of education across SMSAs were added in place of income, its collinear variable, higher failure rates were found to be associated with greater initial levels of education (Table 6.3).

We hypothesized that the performance of black-owned firms should be positively related to their level of human capital since those with large amounts of human capital have demonstrated a willingness to invest time and effort for future returns; and since greater training implies greater ability to manage a business. Our results did not confirm that increasing levels of black adult educational attainment, as one measure of human capital, were helpful either in significantly lowering failure rates of black-owned firms, or in helping firms to form. We found, in fact, that black entrepreneurs in areas with rising levels of education tend to form larger businesses with paid employees at significantly lower rates. In sum, greater education seemed to caution many to stay away from starting new ventures. Moreover, differences in initial levels of education among SMSAs were significantly associated with higher failure rates.

CHANGES IN BLACK PROFESSIONAL AND MANAGERIAL EMPLOYMENT

Areas experiencing increasing levels of black professional and managerial employment were significantly associated with greater number of formations across all firms both with and without paid employees (Tables 6.1 and 6.2). This was particularly true for larger black-owned manufacturing, tranportation, and service establishments, as well as for all smaller firms with no employees in every industry. However, the failure rate of black-owned firms had no significant assocation with rising pools of black professionals and managers, with the exception of retail businesses with paid employees.

We hypothesized two possible, distinct lines of causation concerning the relationship between increasing supplies of black professional and managerial talent and the performance of black-owned firms. Under the first, increased income from outside, alternative employment, coupled with greater opportunities for black professionals and managers, decrease the likelihood of formations of black-owned firms and lower the chances of existing firms continuing. Under the second scenario, increasing pools of black professionals and managers represent the class of individuals who have through their acquisition of human capital demonstrated a willingness to invest for future returns. Consequently, under this human capital hypothesis, we would expect increasing pools of black professionals and managers to be directly related to both the formation of firms and their continuation through time.

The results support the the human capital hypotheses concerning firm formations. The results indicate, first, that greater supplies of those possessing the training and aptitude to seek future rewards translates into larger number of new ventures being formed. The results also indicate, however, that increasing opportunity costs of self-employment in retailing establishments with paid employees are often too high for black entrepreneurs to continue in that business (Table 6.3).

Our theoretical model advanced the argument that areas with higher levels of black self-employed persons per unit of population are areas where relatively more individuals perceive the utility associated with self-employment exceeding that of being a worker. Commensurate with this interpretation, it was further argued that such places would, therefore, reflect fewer perceived obstacles to being self-employed compared to places having lower probabilities of blacks being self-employed.

The results of the empirical investigation confirm that areas with relatively greater initial probablity of black self-empoyment tend, in general, to be associated with greater business formations over time. This holds for firms both with and without paid employees aggregated across all industries (Tables 6.1 and 6.2). Within specific industries, a higher initial percentage of black self-employed persons was positively associated with starting new ventures over subsequent periods in construction, transportation, wholesale, retail and service firms with no paid employees. Among larger firms with paid employees, greater initial probability of black self-employment was, again, directly related to formations in construction, transportation, wholesale and services firms across time.

MARKET WIDENING: PERCENTAGE CHANGE IN BLACK POPULATION

Results indicate that a widening of the market for black business products and services, represented by greater percentage increases in black population, positively impacts the undertaking of new ventures. Greater percentage increases in the black population were positively associated with greater formations of firms both with and without paid employees, aggregated across industries. Market widening also increased formations of large firms in manufacturing, wholesale, retail, service, and finance, insurance and real estate. Percentage increases in black population, however, had no impact on the failure rate of black-owned firms regardless of employment status.

BLACK MEDIAN FAMILY INCOME: MARKET DEPTH, SAVINGS, AND EQUITY

The impact of higher black median family income on black-owned business development seems to tell a consistent story. With the one exception of the construction industry, which will be discussed shortly, areas with higher black median family income tend to be highly associated with the formation of smaller firms with more personalized services and products (Table 6.1). Smaller black-owned firms, consisting mostly of sole proprietorships and partnerships with no employees, in finance, insurance and real estate, and in personal and business services, offer by their very nature a more personalized relationship between consumer and producer than does wholesaling, retailing, and manufacturing. It is not surprising, therefore, that formations of smaller, more personalized businesses in these areas are significantly associated with the depth of the black consumer market in every region. In addition, these type of small, personalized businesses, with no paid employees and low capital requirements, are natural vehicles for personal equity-based ventures. Thus, areas having greater median family income would, therefore, be expected to have greater numbers of such firms being formed from a relatively larger base of personal savings and assets.

Relatedly, among larger firms with paid employees, we observe a significant and positive relationship between greater levels of black middle class income and firm formation only in the business and personal services sector (Table 6.2). The other major point to note concerning firm formation and black median family income is that black middle class areas in the West support not only greater formations of smaller firms in every industry, except construction, but also larger formations in retail, and finance, insurance and real estate (Table 6.1 and 6.2). No other region, outside of the West, has greater levels of black median income stimulating formations of larger firms with paid employees in any industry except for the service industry. Middle class blacks in the West also appear to be more likely to channel savings and equity capital into larger real estate and retail establishments.

The construction industry seems to have a dynamic all its own. It is the only sector which has significantly lower formations associated with higher black median family income everywhere, and across all firm employment categories. Apparently, the depth of black middle class areas, by itself, does not offer a sufficiently strong market for black construction firms to develop; nor do personal equity funds appear to be channelled into construction firms as readily as some other areas since construction is by nature a very highly leveraged industry. It would appear, therefore, that this sector is especially dependent on set-aside programs and other government loan programs.

Taken as a whole, and aggregating across all industries, we note that the market demand supported by black median family income is not associated with lower firm failures anywhere. In fact, higher levels of black median family income are directly associated with greater business failures among all larger firms with paid employees in every region, as well as with small black-owned retail stores everywhere. Thus, overall, greater black income aided in the formation of smaller black businesses, but had no impact on failure rates of smaller black firms with no paid employees. Higher black family income also had no impact on the formation of larger black firms with paid employees in all regions outside the West, but higher black income was associated everywhere with greater firm failure rates of larger black firms.

Areas with greater levels of black median family income were hypothesized as being better able to generate the savings required to start new enterprises. This association was also assumed to hold for the ability to sustain continuations over time since new ventures require periodic capital infusions. We found that higher levels of black median income stimulated the formation of businesses with no paid employees far more than for larger businesses with paid employees. In particular, higher black median income was most significantly associated with the smaller, more equity based, personalized business sectors with low capital requirements. Only in the West did we observe a significant, postive correlation between higher median income and larger new ventures with paid employees. Moreover, higher levels of black median family income were directly associated with failures of smaller firms in sectors which also experienced greater formations with greater levels of income. Black income was, apparently, not of the size to generate the sustained savings needed to impact continuations.

DIFFERENCES IN LEVELS OF RESIDENTIAL SEGREGATION

The impact of greater levels of residential segregation contrasts sharply with the impact of higher levels of black median family income. In contrast to areas with higher levels of median family income, areas with higher levels of residential segregation experience significantly lower formations of new ventures aggregated across all industries. Such areas have less market depth and less available equity capital than higher black median income areas. While lower formations in more segregated communities were most notable in the small retail, service, and finance, insurance and real estate industries, these sectors experienced greater number of formations in higher black income areas across all regions. This was also the case for larger service firms with paid employees. Only in the construction industry do we observe lower formations associated with both higher income and higher residential segregation. In addition, while higher median income was associated with greater failure rates for firms with paid employees, residential segregation had no impact on failure rates of black-owned firms with paid employees. Similarly, while greater black income had no association with failure rates among small firms with no employees, higher residential segregation was associated with greater failure rates among smaller firms.

CHANGES IN THE RATE OF UNEMPLOYMENT

Changes in the rate of unemployment across areas was found to be inversely related to the formation of new black-owned businesses aggregated across all industries in those areas; thus the hypothesis that downturns in the business cycle negatively impact black business formation is largely confirmed. Looking at specific industries, a significant, direct relationship between firm formations and business cycle activity occurred most notably in smaller construction, manufacturing, retail and service firms; and in larger service, wholesale, and construction firms with paid employees. Changes in the unemployment rate were also associated with greater failures among all firms with paid employees, aggregated across all industries. Thus, larger firms with payrolls are most sensitive to business cycle activity.

LOANS FROM BLACK-OWNED BANKS

Surprisingly, both initial loans and increases in loans from black-owned banks were found to be quite significant in lowering the rate of failure among larger black firms with paid employees. Higher initial loans were also found to be moderately significant in lowering the failure rates of smaller black firms with no paid employees. Moreover, both higher initial levels of black bank loans and increases in loans from black-owned banks had some influence on the formation of new ventures in smaller service and transportation firms, as well as larger service firms. These latter types of establishments clearly require less capital than, for instance larger emerging finance, insurance and real estate firms or larger retail establishments with paid employees. Likewise, increases in black bank loans tended to support the start of sole proprietorships and partnerships with no paid employees in finance, insurance, and real estate, but not the formation of larger firms in this sector which, again, presumably have greater capital needs than black banks could satisfy. The evidence also suggests, however, a lack of support for forming larger black-owned retail establishments. In general, these results support the belief that black banks though constrained by they limited size in meeting the capital thresholds of larger, more capital acquisitive businesses, do fulfill a need in helping to form smaller businesses requiring less capital. Furthermore, black banks appear to provide more interim financing for existing black-owned firms than previously realized.

SMALL BUSINESS ADMINISTRATION LOAN PROGRAMS

The sustained SBA investment in the West over the 1971-1977 period, documented in chapter two, resulted in significantly greater impacts on the starting of new black-owned ventures in the West relative to that of any other region. Aggregating across all industries, increases in SBA financing resulted in significant increases in firm formations across all employment size categories in that region. Among smaller firms with no employees, changes in SBA loans in the West (SBAWEST) were directly associated with new formations in manufacturing, transportation, retail, and finance, insurance and real estate. SBA financing in the West was also positively correlated with the formation of larger construction firms in that region, but inversely related to the formation of small construction firms with no employees.

Overall, no other region showed a positive impact of SBA financing on aggregate firm formation across all industries. There were, however, some direct impacts on firm formation in a few specific industries in other regions. These included larger construction and retail establishments with paid employment in the Midwest, as well as both transportation firms, with and without paid employees, and larger retail establishments in the South. On the other hand, changes in SBA loans were inversely related to starting new ventures with paid employees in the service sector in both the Northeast and Midwest. Formations of larger wholesale concerns in the South, and smaller wholesale firms in the Northeast were also inversely related to SBA financing, as were smaller construction firms in the South.

By and large, with the exception of larger black-owned retail establishments in the Northeast, the impact of SBA loan assistance on the failure rates of existing black businesses appears to be of no real significance.

TABLE 6.1

FORMATION OF BLACK-OWNED FIRMS WITH NO PAID EMPLOYEES

	ALL INDUSTRIES	CONSTRUCTION	MANUFACTURING	TRANSPORTATION	WHOLESALE	RETAIL	FINANCE, INSUR., & REAL ESTATE	SERVICES
BLKEDIF	-2.38 (1.67)	-.396** (.191)	-.192*** (.063)	-.191 (.247)	.089** (.044)	-1.36** (.542)	.246 (.235)	-.568 (1.03)
PRMNDIF	.181*** (.029)	.0166*** (.0034)	.462E-02*** (.112E-02)	.731E-02* (.437E-02)	.355E-02*** (.078E-02)	.041*** (.010)	.0122*** (.004)	.101*** (.018)
SELFEM72	.217*** (.056)	.0271*** (.0064)	.231E-02 (.213E-02)	.028*** (.008)	.257E-02* (.147E-02)	.034* (.018)	-.720E-04 (78.0E-04)	.123*** (.034)
BBLNDIF	.072 (.055)	.576E-02 (.627E-02)	-.444E-03 (2.08E-03)	.020** (.008)	-.243E-03 (1.44E-03)	.527E-02 (1.78E-02)	.0130* (.0076)	.028 (.034)
BBLNSQ	-.253E-03 (2.97E-03)	-.182E-03 (.230E-03)	-.747E-04 (1.10E-04)	-.707E-03* (.430E-03)	.735E-05 (7.73E-05)	-.231E-03 (.970E-03)	-.454E-03 (.420E-03)	-.890E-03 (1.84E-03)
BLN72	.049** (.028)	-.229E-02 (.323E-02)	.783E-03 (1.07E-03)	.757E-02* (.417E-02)	-.726E-03 (.740E-03)	.102E-02 (.917E-02)	.603E-02 (.396E-02)	.0368** (.0174)
SBAWEST	.055** (.025)	-.546E-02** (.284E-02)	.319E-02*** (.095E-02)	.780E-02** (.367E-02)	.612E-03 (.650E-03)	.019** (.008)	.903E-02*** (.349E-02)	.020 (.015)
SBANE	-.031 (.036)	-.506E-02 (.416E-02)	-.458E-04 (13.8E-04)	.461E-02 (.538E-02)	-.322E-02*** (.095E-02)	-.850E-03 (11.8E-03)	-.361E-02 (.511E-02)	-.023 (.022)
SBANC	-.555E-03 (14.2E-03)	.991E-04 (16.3E-04)	.414E-03 (.540E-03)	-.153E-02 (.210E-02)	.151E-03 (.370E-03)	-.377E-02 (.463E-02)	.288E-04 (20.0E-04)	.405E-02 (.877E-02)
SBASO	-.0114 (.0361)	-.706E-02* (.415E-02)	-.144E-02 (.138E-02)	.936E-02* (.536E-02)	.646E-03 (.950E-03)	.014 (.011)	-.119E-02 (.509E-02)	-.026 (.022)

TABLE 6.1 (CONT.)

	ALL INDUSTRIES	CONSTRUCTION	MANUFACTURING	TRANSPORTATION	WHOLESALE	RETAIL	FINANCE, INSUR., & REAL ESTATE	SERVICES
BLKPCH	8.93*** (2.07)	.0196 (.2376)	.123* (.075)	.050 (.307)	.146*** (.054)	2.21*** (.674)	1.37*** (.291)	5.02*** (1.28)
WSTBFAMIN	.112E-02*** (.015E-02)	-.352E-04** (.166E-04)	.130E-04** (.055E-04)	.805E-04*** (.215E-04)	.112E-04*** (.038E-04)	.190E-03*** (.050E-03)	.193E-03*** (.020)	.662E-03*** (.090E-03)
NEBFAMIN	.610E-03*** (.150E-03)	-.425E-04** (.167E-04)	.521E-05 (.554E-05)	.820E-04*** (.214E-04)	.113E-04*** (.038E-04)	.453E-04 (.472E-04)	.970E-04*** (.205E-04)	.412E-03*** (.089E-03)
NCBFAMIN	.643E-03*** (.130E-03)	-.283E-04** (.150E-04)	.105E-05 (.508E-05)	.893E-04*** (.198E-04)	.337E-05 (.351E-05)	.556E-04 (.400E-04)	.104E-03*** (.019E-03)	.418E-03*** (.080E-03)
SOBFAMIN	.770E-03*** (.180E-03)	-.227E-04 (.200E-04)	.715E-05 (.671E-05)	.965E-04*** (.261E-04)	.606E-05 (.463E-05)	.737E-04 (.574E-04)	.128E-03** (.025E-03)	.482E-03*** (.110E-03)
SEGRE72	-.035*** (.009)	-.200E-02* (.109E-02)	-.447E-03 (.360E-03)	-.801E-03 (1.41E-03)	-.227(E-04) (2.50E-04)	-.564E-02* (.309E-02)	-.289E-02** (.134E-02)	-.023*** (.006)
UNEMPDIF	-.160** (.090)	-.0170* (.0100)	-.776E-02** (.350E-02)	.019 (.014)	.193E-02 (.241E-02)	-.048* (.029)	-. 471E-02 (1.29E-02)	-.104* (.056)
R^2	.75	.37	.49	.32	.48	.62	.75	.72
F	21.30	4.14	6.70	3.32	6.38	11.74	20.66	18.30

*** Significant at .01 level

** Significant at .05 level

* Significant at .10 level

TABLE 6.2

FORMATION OF BLACK-OWNED FIRMS WITH PAID EMPLOYEES

	ALL INDUSTRIES	CONSTRUCTION	MANUFACTURING	TRANSPORTATION	WHOLESALE	RETAIL	FINANCE, INSUR.., & REAL ESTATE	SERVICES
BLKEDIF	-1.072*** (.330)	-.0502 (.096)	.0713 (.049)	-.173*** (.066)	.039 (.026)	-.236 * (.150)	.055 (.038)	-.778 *** (.205)
PRMNDIF	.0266*** (.006)	-.725E-03 (1.69E-03)	.392E-02*** (.008E-02)	.252E-02** (.116E-02)	-.699E-05 (47.0E-05)	.136E-02 (.266E-02)	.233E-03 (.680E-03)	.0193*** (.0036)
SELFEM72	.0457*** (.0112)	.0112*** (.0032)	.118E-02 (.166E-02)	.437E-02 ** (.220E-02)	231E-02*** (.088E-02)	.457E-02 (.504E-02)	.533E-03 (1.28E-03)	.0216*** (.0069)
BRLNDIF	.0104 (.0109)	237E-02 (.314E-02)	.143E-03 (1.63E-03)	-.773E-02 (2.15E-02)	-.424E-03 (.860E-03)	-.153E-02 (.493E-02)	-.227E-02** (.125E-02)	.0129** (.0067)
BBLNSQ	-.665E-03 (.600E-03)	-.272E-03 * (.160E-03)	-.611E-04 (.900E-04)	-.916E-04 (1.20E-04)	.700E-04 (.470E-04)	.152E-03 (.270E-03)	.791E-04 (.700E-04)	-.540E-03 (.370E-03)
BLN72	.808E-03 (5.63E-03)	-.610E-03 (1.62E-03)	-.564E-03 (.840E-03)	.727E-03 (1.11E-03)	-.187E-03 (.450E-03)	-.425E-02 * (.254E-02)	-.721E-03 (.640E-03)	.641E-2** (.346E-02)
SBAWEST	.0103** (.0049)	411E-02*** (.142E-02)	.562E-03 (.740E-03)	.259E-03 (.980E-03)	.131E-03 (.390E-03)	.197E-02 (.224E-02)	.647E-03 (.570E-03)	.265E-02 (.205E-02)
SBANE	-.899E-02 (.726E-02)	-.495E-03 (2.09E-03)	-.137E-02 (.108E-02)	-.109E-02 (.143E-02)	.336E-03 (.570E-03)	.208E-02 (.328E-02)	-.595E-04 (8.20E-04)	-.839E-02** (.447E-02)
SBANC	.143E-02 (.284E-02)	.136E-02* (.080E-02)	.975E-04 (4.20E-04)	.775E-03 (.560E-03)	.115E-03 (.220E-03)	.246E-02** (.127E-02)	-.627E-04 (3.30E-04)	-.332E-02** (.175E-02)
SBASO	-.328E-02 (.723E-02)	-.313E-02 (.208E-02)	-.117E-02 (.108E-02)	.226E-02* (.140E-02)	-.111E-02 ** (.055E-02)	.536E-02** (.326E-02)	.911E-03 (.820E-03)	-.639E-02 (.445E-02)

TABLE 6.2

	ALL INDUSTRIES	CONSTRUCTION	MANUFACTURING	TRANSPORTATION	WHOLESALE	RETAIL	FINANCE, INSUR., & REAL ESTATE	SERVICES
BLKPCH	1.122*** (.414)	.273** (.119)	.120** (.061)	-.123 (.081)	-.0259 (.0328)	.155 (.187)	.096** (.047)	.627** (.254)
WSTBFAMIN	.123E-03*** (.030E-03)	-.167E-04** (.083E-04)	.327E-05 (.753E-05)	.819E-05 (.573E-05)	.337E-05 (.229E-05)	.298E-04** (.131E-04)	.756E-05** (.333E-05)	.879E-04*** (.200E-04)
NEBFAMIN	.199E-05 (3.00E-05)	-.302E-04*** (.080E-04)	.222E-05 (.432E-05)	-.135E-05 (.570E-05)	.827E-07 (26.0E-07)	-.353E-05 (1.32E-05)	.273E-05 (.333E-05)	.320E-04** (.170E-04)
NCBFAMIN	.298E-04 (.267E-04)	-.244E-04*** (.076E-04)	.987E-07 (31.2E-07)	-.203E-06 (6.41E-06)	-.558E-06 (2.10E-06)	.899E-05 (1.20E-05)	.458E-05 (.305E-05)	.412E-04*** (.160E-04)
SOBFAMIN	.496E-04 (.370E-04)	-.212E-04** (.100E-04)	.348E-05 (1.00E-05)	.272E-05 (1.20E-05)	.800E-06 (2.79E-06)	.655E-05 (2.00E-05)	.464E-05 (.403E-05)	.526E-04*** (.200E-04)
SEGRE72	-.595E-02** (.190E-02)	-.132E-02** (.055E-02)	-.548E-03** (.280E-03)	-.138E-03 (.370E-03)	-.140E-03 (.150E-03)	.105E-02 (.086E-02)	.116E-03 (.220E-03)	-.497E-02*** (.117E-02)
UNEMPDIF	-.0491*** (.0183)	-.970E-02* (.527E-02)	-.285E-02 (.272E-02)	-.508E-03 (3.62E-03)	-.225E-02* (.137E-02)	-.829E-02 (.829E-02)	.138E-02 (.210E-02)	-.0269** (.0113)
R^2	.70	.46	.30	.29	.26	.32	.20	.70
F	16.23	5.92	3.03	2.84	2.42	3.31	1.73	16.16

*** Significant at .01 level

** Significant at .05 level

* Significant at .10 level

TABLE 6.3   FAILURE RATE OF BLACK-OWNED FIRMS

	ALL FIRMS, NO EMPLOYEES (LOG)	RETAIL FIRMS, NO EMPLOYEES	ALL FIRMS, WITH EMPLOYEES (LOG)	RETAIL FIRMS, WITH EMPLOYEES
BLKEDIF	-.058 (.083)	.092 (7.53)	-.078 (.196)	-7.07 (15.3)
PRMNDIF	.208E-02 (.147E-02)	-.077 (.133)	.163E-02 (.346E-02)	.870 *** (.271)
SELFEM72	-.337E-02 (.279E-02)	.134 (.252)	-.323E-02 (.655E-02)	-.274 (.513)
BBLNDIF	-.341E-02 (.273E-02)	-.084 (.246)	-.014 ** (.006)	-.350 (.502)
BBLNSQ	.027E-03 (.150E-03)	-.075E-01 (.134E-01)	.073E-02 ** (.035E-02)	-.015E-01 (.273E-01)
BLN72	-.245E-02 * (.140E-02)	-.057 (.127)	-.011 *** (.003)	-.175 (.259)
SBAWEST	-.018E-01 (.012E-01)	-.035E-01 (1.12E-01)	-.044E-01 (.029E-01)	-.239 (.228)
SBANE	-.021E-01 (.018E-01)	-.189 (.175)	-.041E-01 (.043E-01)	-.640 ** (.334)
SBANC	-.022E-02 (.071E-02)	-.043 (.064)	.026E-01 (.016E-01)	.164 (.131)
SBASO	.026E-03 (1.80E-03)	.062 (.163)	.029E-01 (.042E-01)	.098 (.332)
BLKPCH	.088 (.103)	-4.59 (9.36)	.202 (.243)	-28.9 (19.0)
WSTBFAMIN	.079E-04 (.100E-04)	.260E-02 *** (.066E-02)	.040E-03 *** (.017E-03)	.018E-01 (.013E-01)
NEBFAMIN	.072E-04 (.100E-04)	.010E-02 *** (.030E-02)	.042E-03*** (.017E-03)	.010E-01 (.013E-01)
NCBFAMIN	.056E-04 (.066E-04)	.022E-01 *** (.006E-01)	.035E-03 ** (.015E-03)	.069E-02 (.123E-02)
SOBFAMIN	.051E-05 (1.00E-05)	.021E-01 *** (.008E-01)	.046E-03 ** (.020E-03)	.012E-01 (.016E-01)
SEGRE72	.800E-03 * (.450E-03)	-.036 (.043)	.045E-03 (1.11E-03)	-.014 (.087)
UNEMPDIF	-.020E-01 (.046E-01)	-.560 (.414)	.017 * (.010)	.571 (.843)
R^2	.23	.30	.22	.21
F	2.08	3.06	1.97	1.90

Chapter VII

CONCLUSIONS AND POLICY IMPLICATIONS

This research has attempted to quantitatively analyze the impact of opportunity costs, capital access and availability, market factors, business human capital, and other overall macro conditions on black-own firm formation and firm failure. The theoretical framework of this study explored how these factors exert themselves via entrepreneurial decisions to start or continue in business. The study did not seek to prove or demonstrate whether such factors as public and private institutional financial capital, equity capital, extent and variability of market demand, and human capital are important to business development since their importance to economic and business development has long been established and repeatedly confirmed. The importance of such factors is axiomatic. Rather, we sought to examine to what degree and along what lines they are operative in black business development, and whether they are of the magnitude and stability to significantly impact black-own firm development and continuation.

Controlling for size of firm, by having separate equations for small black enterprises with no employees, and for larger black firms with paid employees, we found that, overall, macro variables were not a good predictor of black-owned firm failure rates. This suggests that black firm failure rates are probably more directly associated with individual characteristics of entrepreneurs, themselves, than with overall differences among metropolitan areas. However, the fact that small business failure rates are statistically indistinquishable among all ethnic

171

groups strongly suggests that small firms probably fail for largely the same reasons across all groups. This fact, by itself, seriously calls into question the impression, held by some previous researchers, that blacks are somehow less able and less qualified to run businesses than other groups.

Previous overemphasis of simply studying failure rates and loan delinquency rates of black businesses assisted through the SBA Economic Opportunity Loan program, cited in some of the studies mentioned in chapters three and five, has only added to this misunderstanding. Such loans were designed strickly to aid "disadvantaged" borrowers with little or no business experience or training. Moreover, these loans were found to be much "weaker" than SBA loans generally and were used largely to finance high risk, small retail and small, low-skilled personal service firms.[1] Studies using this type of sample design would inevitably find very high failure rates for any ethnic group.

The finding that greater supplies of black professionals and managers working in large corporations are largely complementary to black business formations is quite important. The dissemination of technical assistance programs like the Urban Leàgue's black executive outreach programs, the Interracial Council of Business Opportunity, black-based business leagues, and other similar conduits for black professional and managerial support and assistance to black-owned firms, both formal and informal, have apparently been quite instrumental in aiding in the formation of black firms. This suggests that public policy should continue to encourage affirmative action programs in order to provide expanding managerial training grounds.

Recent work has also comfirmed that part-time self-employment has become vitally important to the growth dynamic of minority enterprise. Overall, minority "part-timers" have been found to be better educated, younger and most likely to be in the emerging fields of finance, insurance, and real estate and most lines of skill-intensive professional services.[2] Most of these higher skilled, highly educated part-time entrepreneurs come from the pool of minority professionals and managers working in the corporate environment.

The finding that black-owned commercial banks have been important in sustaining black firms, while they have been of less help in providing start-up capital also has several policy implications. In many ways the limited impact of black-owned commercial banks on black business formation parallels the limitations in black-own business development generally. The performance of black commercial banks is greatly limited by their size which, in turn, is directly related to their limited black patronage, and the magnitude and stability of the income and employment of those patrons. Recent research has confirmed that black banks incurr disproportionately larger losses during recessions due to the lack of wealth of their clients and the disproportionate income losses among blacks during a recession.[3] Because of the low and volatile income of its depositors, black banks have significantly lower average deposit account sizes than non-minority banks and very high variability in these deposits. Moreover, because of their very large deposit variability, black banks must remain much more liquid than commercial banks in general.[4]

In addition, it is widely recognized that the fraction of black banks' total deposits accounted for by U.S. government deposits is larger than that held by non-minority banks. Government regulations, moreover, require that such deposits be held in highly liquid forms, most notably in U.S. government securities. Due to these two factors, high liquidity and reliance on U.S. government funds, black commercial bank lending ability is greatly constrained by the particular financial environment in which they must operate. If black-owned banks, therefore, are to have greater impact on urban economic development through the financing of black business enterprises then some outside help is needed in terms of existing loan participation and loan insurance programs being maintained, at a minimum, and expanded, if at all possible. Government assistance in this area can expand both directly and indirectly through appropriate linkages with the private sector. In this regard, former Congressman Parren Mitchell of Maryland has recommended that thought should be given to federal tax legislation that would permit larger institutions with pools of capital to be given tax write-offs for joint capital sharing ventures with minority financial institutions.[5]

SBA loan guarantees are granted to black businesses through both non-minority as well as minority banks. But care must be taken not to have SBA policy and some aspects of general monetary policy, conflicting with the real needs and interest of minority businesses. In late 1974, for instance, the maximum allowable interest rate of SBA loans was less than the going rate of federal funds sold, a nearly riskless asset.[6] All banks, therefore, had a reduced incentive to grant SBA loans, thereby depressing the business loans to assets ratio. Since newer black banks participate in government loan insurance programs at a greater rate than other banks, the high opportunity cost of participation was a disproportionate hindrance to black bank loan programs.

The SBA threshold implications of this study suggest that greater amounts of SBA funds should be directed toward larger employment generating firms, rather than the present low levels of funding to smaller, nonemployment generating firms with low capital needs. Relatedly, better, more equitable distribution of SBA funds across regions are also needed. The South, in particular, has been systematically underrepresented by SBA funds to black businesses despite the fact that the South has 55 percent of the total black population , and the lowest failure rates of black-owned businesses among all regions. While this flies in the face of conventional wisdom, in fact, it is only in the South were we observe a positive correlation between the probability of blacks being self-employed and the depth of market. These two facts suggest that while overall black business performance is, on average, strongest in the West, the entrepreneurial decision process in the South is on par with any other region despite its relatively poor SBA representation.

Findings from this study also call attention to the critical issue of black firms relying solely on black patronage. Our findings that greater black median income only aids in the formation of small, personalized black-owned enterprises, while being directly associated with greater failure rates of larger, employment generating black enterprises, parallels the fact that black-owned businesses are drawing a declining share of the black consumers' $200 billion a year market. The percentage of black disposable income going to black-owned companies dropped from 13.5 percent of black income in 1969 to 7 percent in 1984, or a near 50 percent reduction over the past fifteen years.[7] Moreover, black companies in the retail sector now face competition from mass marketing majority retail firms in areas that were once a nearly exclusive market for black retailers. Black hair products, for instance, used to be the exclusive province of black-owned hair companies. Now, 70 percent of black hair products are sold by Revlon and Alberta-Culver.[8] While there have been several optimistic projections concerning black-owned businesses' ability to penetrate the larger general market, until increased market penetration in the general population becomes a reality; and unless the trend of black disposable income comprising a declining market base for black business products is reversed, the future of the black-owned business sector as a definable entity does not bode well.

Both the theoretical model presented in this research and the findings concerning the impact of black median income on smaller equity-based businesses, suggest that vehicles which can increase the equity or net worth position of black-own businesses would greatly lower the risk and opportunity cost for qualified black persons choosing entrepreneurship. This can be supported in two ways: (i) through macro policies which aid in the stability and growth of black family income as a source of primary savings for equity investment, and (ii) through programs designed to impact the equity position of black businesses directly. Though we have argued for better designed SBA programs, it must be observed that in several instances SBA loans have often exacerbated the problem of excessive, long-term liability by sustaining higher loan interest payment obligations of black businesses. The Minority Enterprise Small Business Investment Company program (MESBIC), which was originally designed to provide venture capital by taking an equity position in newly formed minority firms, has simply not worked well. Virtually every study on this subject has indicated that MESBICs have not invested significantly in minority firms and that the little that has been invested in minority businesses has been extended almost entirely as loans, thereby increasing the long-term debt position of many companies which end in default.[9] There is a critical need for a solid, workable MESBIC program along its original lines and purpose. This need for equity investments in promising minority enterprises is also highlighted by the fact that recent micro evidence clearly shows that even the most profitable minority firms are undercaptialized and carry substantially heavier debt structure than their non-minority counterparts of equal size.

Our finding concerning the negative relationship between increases in black adult educational attainment and formation of black-owned firms should be interpreted with some caution. Black adult education in the SMSAs included in this study increased from 10.05 to 10.30 years over the 1970 to 1980 period. Our

176

model, in particular, assessed the impact of SMSAs which had black adult educational increases in excess of this average increase. While this gives a fair test to the importance of actual increases in average years of educational attainment, it cannot, by itself, thoroughly represent the importance of significant educational advances on black business development. Recent evidence on the significant decline of black male enrollment in post-secondary education only highlights this problem. Moreover, the impact of human resource development in this area cannot be assessed by simply measuring small increases in time of enrollment, but rather by the impact of greater enrollment in the administrative sciences and in quantitative and engineering curricular and by increased educational quality over an extended period of time. This kind of information, which would also retrieve cohort effects, could not be determined by assessing years of educational change over such a short period of time. In this light, it should be reemphasized that differentials in the long-run attainment of total years of black adult education across metropolitan areas were found to be positively associated with black firm formation across areas. As more extensive time series data on black-own firms become available, it should be possible to better evaluate this impact.

Information from the bivariate correlations was also quite suggestive. Both residential segregation and high concentrations of black population were negatively associated with black business formation, while higher black family income (depth of market) and greater increases in black population (wider markets) were positively associated with black business formation. Nonetheless, while wider and deeper markets were judged to be more beneficial to black business development than heavily concentrated, segregated areas, higher levels of black self-employed persons in the non-South were (i) positively related to residential segregation and population concentration, but (ii) negatively related to deeper markets everywhere but in the South, and (iii) not related at all to wider markets.   Only in the South were there are no disjunctions between market depth, market width, residential segregation and black population concentration. Likewise, only in the South do we observe the probability of black self-employment being positively related to the black median income; and only in the South do we observe positive correlations between both concentrations of black population and black median family income, and residential segregation and black median family income. These facts, along with the relatively lower black firm failures in the South, shown in chapter II, table 2.4, suggest that the process of black business development and the nature of entrepreneurial choice may be somewhat different in that region.

There is, therefore, a need for potential and existing black businessmen, particularly outside the South, to better recognize and assess those market factors which improve the likelihood of continuing in business. Where there is disjunction between the two, deeper and wider markets should be emphasized over more segregated and concentrated markets. These latter markets rely too heavily on the continuance of small, largely unprofitable retail and service businesses. While maintainance of the small retail and service sectors is often critical for residentially segregated communities, and should be supported in those communities, it must be understood that growth and expansion of the black-owned business sector requires the harnessing of those forces which promote growth of larger firms in more advanced sectors.[10]

Putting aside for the moment the importance of equity capital and other financial capital, which we have already discussed, if the policy objective is to increase business formations then the evidence indicates that, (i) promoting opportunities for larger numbers of black professionals and managers is largely complementary to the black firm formation process, (ii) harnessing wider markets of increased black support implies that black firms must serve several locations where blacks reside, and not just one or two highly concentrated areas, (iii) maintaining and increasing black family income is fundamental, and (iv) business development should be promoted in areas having high levels of black educational attainment as a correlate to black professional and managerial development. However, we have also seen that increases in these variables have not yet proven to be sufficient in overcoming the low formation rates of black-own business. Moreover, it is clear that increasing overall black business participation still requires devising strategies which both lower failure rates and increase firm formation rates simultaneously. The fact that black per capita business formations are lower while business failures are comparable to other racial/ethnic groups still translates to a higher ratio of failures relative to formations. Our results suggest that unless this ratio is lowered significantly, then both the perceived and actual real risks of blacks being self-employed will continue to be high.

NOTES

Chapter I

[1]The Office of Minority Business Enterprise (OMBE) was changed to the Minority Business Development Agency (MBDA) in 1980.

[2]See William F. Haddad and G. Douglas Pugh, editors, Black Economic Development, The American Assembly, Columbia University (Englewood Cliffs: Prentice Hall, 1969).

[3]Sole proprietorship, partnership and corporation data based on Statistics of Income. Business Income Tax Returns, and Corporation Income Tax Returns 1972, 1977 and 1982 (Statistics Division of the Internal Revenue Service). Minority-owned business statistics taken from the 1972, 1977 and 1982 Survey of Minority-Owned Enterprises (Washington, D.C.: U.S. Department of Commerce, Bureau of the Census, 1975; 1980; 1985).

[4]The State of Small Business: A Report to the President, "Minority-Owned Business," Appendix C (Washington, D.C.: U.S. Government Printing Office, 1983) p. 301.

[5]Richard Stevens, "Measuring Minority Business Formation and Failure," Review of Black Political Economy, Vol. 12, No. 4, Spring 1984, p. 75.

[6]1982 Survey of Minority-Owned Business Enterprises, U.S. Department of Commerce, Bureau of the Census (Washington, D.C.: U.S. Government Printing Office); and Richard Stevens and Norman Hurwitz, "A Review and Critique of the 1977 Survey of Minority-Owned Enterprises" (Washington, D.C.: U.S. Department of Commerce, Minority Business Development Agency, February, 1982).

[7]Other empirical studies in this area include, Faith Ando and Robin Sickles, An Analysis of Growth and Failure Rates of Minority-Owned Business (Washington, D.C.: Minority Business Development Agency (MBDA), U.S. Department of Commerce, September, 1983); Timothy Bates, Antonio Furino, and Richard Wadsworth, New Perspectives on Minority Business Development (Development Through Applied Science, San Antonio, TX., August, 1983); Peter Bearse, An Econometric Analysis of Minority Entrepreneurship (Washington, D.C.: MBDA, U.S. Department of Commerce, September, 1983); and John Handy and David Swinton, The Determinants of Growth of Black - Owned Businesses (MBDA, U.S. Department of Commerce, September, 1983). Only the study by Handy and Swinton looks specifically into black-owned businesses across SMSAs.

[8]Timothy Bates and Antonio Furino, New Perspectives on Minority Business Development: A Study of Minority Business Potential Using the MBDA Financial Research Data Base (U.S. Department of Commerce, Minority Business Development Agency, August, 1983).

[9]Federal Procurement Data Center, Special Report 401A, 8 April, 1983. Also in The State of Small Business: A Report of the President, Appendix B

(Washington, D.C.: U.S. Government Printing Office, March, 1984) Table B.4, p. 384.

Chapter II

[1]The State of Small Business: A Report to the President, "Minority-Owned Business," Chapter 6 (Washington, D.C.: U.S. Government Printing Office, 1987) p. 225.

[2]Formation (failure) rates were computed by dividing the number of formations (failures) between 1972 and 1977 by the number of firms in the base year (1972). These rates were then divided by five to obtain an annual average rate.

[3]Timothy Bates, "Profitability in Traditional and Emerging Lines of Black Business Enterprise, Journal of Urban Economics (April, 1978); Andrew Brimmer and Henry Terrell, "The Economic Potential of Black Capitalism" Public Policy, 19 (Spring, 1971); Frederic Case, Black Capitalism: Problems in Development (New York, Praeger Publishers, 1972); and Flournoy Coles, Black Economic Development (Nelson Hall Company, 1975).

[4]For two excellent discussions on the history of black business in the United States see Roy F. Lee, The Setting for Black Business Development, Chapter IV (Ithaca, New York: New York State School of Industrial and Labor Relations, Cornell University, 1973); and Robert Kinzer and Edward Sagarin, The Negro In American Business (New York: Greenberg, 1950).

[5]Rashi Fein, "An Economic and Social Profile of the Negro American," in The Negro American, edited by Talcott Parsons and Kenneth Clark (Boston: Beacon Press, 1966); Herbert Northrup and Richard Rowen, Negro Employment in Basic Industry, A Study of Racial Policies in Six Industries (University of Pennsylvania, Wharton School of Finance and Commerce, 1970); Richard Freeman Black Elite (New York: McGraw Hill, 1976); and Sar Levitan, William Johnson and Robert Taggart, Still a Dream: The Changing Status of Blacks Since 1960 (Cambridge: Harvard University Press, 1975).

[6]Timothy Bates, The Nature of the Growth Dynamic in Emerging Lines of Minority Enterprise: Human Capital and Financial Capital Considerations (Washington, D.C.: Government Printing Office, September, 1983); and T. Bates and A. Furino, New Perspectives on Minority Business Development: A Study of Minority Business Potential Using the MDBA Financial Research Data Base, Development Through Applied Science (DETAS), (U.S. Department of Commerce, Minority Business Development Agency, August, 1983).

[7]The State of Small Business: A Report to the President, "Minority-Owned Business," Appendix B (Washington, D.C.: U.S. Government Printing Office, 1984) p. 371.

[8]The State of Small Business, p. 383; and Bates, The Nature of the Growth Dynamic in Emerging Lines of Minority Enterprise, pp. 10, 17, and 65.

[9]Bates, The Nature of the Growth Dynamic, pp. 1-4 and 65.

[10]Ibid., pp. 1-4 and 65.

[11]William Scott, Antonio Furino and Eugene Rodriquez, Key Business Ratios for Minority-Owned Businesses - Analysis and Policy Implications (San Antonio: University of Texas at San Antonio, January, 1981).

[12]The first observation of the relationship between firm size and failure rates for all firms was conducted by David Birch and Susan McCracken. Corporate Evolution: A Micro-Based Analysis (Washington, D.C.: Small Business Administration, January, 1981).

[13]Richard Stevens, "Measuring Minority Business Formation and Failure," (Washington, D.C.: U.S. Department of Commerce, Minority Business Development, December, 1983): 19.

[14]The coefficient of variation is a quick and convenient way of judging a variable's variability or stability. It is equal to the ratio of the standard deviation to the mean. For a discussion of this concept see Taro Yamane, Statistics (New York: Harper and Row); also Harry McAllister Business and Economic Statistics (New York: Wiley and Sons, 1975): 65-66.

Chapter III

[1]Gavin Chen and Richard Stevens, "Minority-Owned Business Problems and Opportunities: A 1983 Update," (U.S. Department of Commerce, Minority Business Development Agency, June, 1984): 2.

[2]Timothy Bates and William Bradford, Financing Black Economic Development (New York: Academic Press, 1979).

[3]Andrew Brimmer, "The Negro in the National Economy." Race and Poverty edited by J. H. Kain (Englewood Cliffs: Prentice Hall, 1969): 89-100.

[4]Don Markwalder, "The Potential for Black Business," The Review of Black Political Economy (Vol. 3, No. 1 (Fall, 1981): 87-93.

[5]Henry Wallich, "The Negro Economy," Newsweek, 70, 1967.

[6]Andrew Brimmer and Henry Terrell, "The Economic Potential of Black Capitalism," Public Policy, 19 (Spring, 1971): 289-328.

[7]Paul Ong, "Factors Influencing the Size of the Black Business Community," The Review of Black Political Economy, Vol. 11, No. 3 (Spring, 1981): 313-319.

[8]John Handy and David Swinton, "The Determinants of the Growth of Black-Owned Businesses: A Preliminary Analysis," Review of Black Political Economy, Vol. 12, No. 4 (Winter, 1984): 85-110.

[9]Bates and Bradford, op. cit.

[10]Timothy Bates, Black Capitalism: A Quantitative Analysis (New York: Praeger, 1973 a); also Timothy Bates, "An Econometric Analysis of Lending to Black Businesses," Review of Economics and Statistics Vol. 55, No. 3 (August, 1973b): 272-283; also Timothy Bates, "Further Comment: Capital Markets and the Potential of Black Entrepreneurship," Public Policy, Vol. 16, No. 2 (Summer, 1978a): 447-449.

[11]John Dominquez, Capital Flows in Minority Areas (Lexington, MA: Lexington Books, 1976).

[12]Alfred Osborne and Michael Granfield, "The Potential of Black Capitalism in Perspective," Public Policy, Vol. 24, No. 4 (Fall, 1976): 529-544.

[13]William Hunter and Joseph Sinkley, "A Socially Optimal Subsidization Model for Inducing Commercial Banks to Participate in Minority Business Development" (Athens, GA: University of Georgia, 1980).

[14]Paul Ong, op. cit.

[15]Harding Young and James Hund, "Negro Entrepreneurship in Southern Economic Development" in Black Americans and White Business, edited by Epstein and Hampton (Encino, CA: Dickenson Publishing Co., 1971): 240-264.

[16]Peter Bearse, An Econometric Analysis of Minority Entrepreneurship (Washington, D.C.: Minority Business (Development Agency, September, 1983).

[17]Timothy Bates, Antonio Furino and Richard Wadsworth, New Perspectives on Minority Business Development: A Study of Minority Business Potential Using the MBDA Financial Research Data Base. (San Antonio, TX: Development Through Applied Science (DETAS), August, 1983).

[18]Samuel Doctors and Sharon Lockwood, "New Directions for Minoirty Enterprise," Law and Contemporary Problems (Winter, 1971).

[19]Timothy Bates, "Effectiveness of the Small Business Administration in Financing Minority Business," The Review of Black Political Economy, Vol. 11, No. 3 (Spring, 1981): 321-336.

[20]Bates and Bradford, op. cit.

[21]Samuel Doctors and Richard Wokutch, "SBA Regional Loan Distribution to Minorities, Review of Black Political Economy, Vol. 11, No. 4 (Summer, 1982):

[22]Robert Yancy, Feberal Government and Black Enterprise (Ballinger Publishing Company, 1974).

[23]Bates and Bradford, op. cit.

[24]Andrew Brimmer, "The Black Banks: An Assessment of Performance and Prospects," Journal of Finance, Vol. 26, No. 2 (May, 1971): 379-405; also Andrew Brimmer, "Recent Developments in Black Banking, 1970-71," Review of Black Political Economy, Vol. 3, 1972.

[25]Edward Irons, "Black Banking -- Problems and Prospects," Journal of Finance, Vol. 26, No. 2 (May, 1971): 407-425.

[26]John Boorman, New Minority-Owned Commercial Banks (Washington, D.C.: Federal Deposit Insurance Corporation, 1973); also John Boorman, "The Prospects for Minority-Owned Commercial Banks: A Comparative Performance Analysis," Journal of Bank Research, 1974.

[27]Eugene Foley, "The Negro Businessman in Search of a Tradition," in The Negro American, edited by Talcott Parsons and Kenneth Clark (Boston: Beacon Press, 1969): 555-592.

[28]Flournoy Coles, An Analysis of Black Entrepreneurship in Seven Urban Areas (Washington, D.C.: The National Business League, 1969).

[29]William Strang, "Minority Economic Development: The Problem of Business Failures. Law and Contemporary Problems, Vol. 36, 1971.

[30]Andrew Brimmer, 1969, op. cit.

[31]Frederic Case, Black Captalism: Problems in Development, (New York: Praeger Publishers, 1972).

[32]William Scott, Antonio Furino, and Eugene Rodriquez, Key Business Ratios for Minority-Owned Businesses: Analysis and Policy Implications (Center for Studies in Business, Economics and Human Resources, College of Business, Unviersity of texas at San Antonio, January, 1981).

[33]Chen and Stevens, op. cit.

[34]Timothy Bates, The Nature of the Growth Dynamic in Emerging Lines of Minority Enterprise: Human Capital and Financial Capital Considerations (Washgington, D.C.: Minority Business Development Agency, September, 1983).

[35]Handy and Swinton, 1983, op. cit.; also John Handy and David Swinton, The Determinants of the Growth of Black-Owned Business: A Preliminary Analysis (Washington, D.C.: U.S. Department of Commerce, Minority Business Development Agency, September, 1983).

[36]Theodore Cross, Black Capitalism, Strategy for Business in the Ghetto (New York: Atheneum, 1969); also Theodore Cross, "A White Paper on Black Capitalism" (Boston: Warren, Gorham and Lamont, Inc., 1971).

[37]Roy Lee. The Setting for Black Business Development (Ithaca, NY: Cornell Unviersity, School of Industrial and Labor Relations, 1973).

[38]Robert Glover, Minority Business Enterprise in Construction (New York: Praeger Press, 1977).

[39]James Lowery and Associates, A New Strategy for Minority Business Enterprise Development (Washington, D.C.: U.S. Department of Commerce, Final Report F1893J4, April, 1979).

[40]Esau Jackson and Stephanie King "Black Business: Review of Problems and Prospects" (Ann Arbor, MI: Bureau of Business Research, University of Michigan, 1972).

[41]Cross, 1971, op. cit., p.27.

[42]Brimmer and Terrell, op. cit.

[43]Brimmer, 1969, op. cit.

[44]Coles, 1969, op. cit; also Flourney Coles, Black Economic Development (Nelson Hall Company, 1975).

[45]Foley, op. cit.

[46]Jackson and King, op. cit.

[47]William Strang, "The Mix of Black Business: Implication for Growth," Business Horizons, No. 62, 1977.

[48]Faith Ando and Robin Sickles, An Analysis of Growth and Failure Rates of Minority-Owned Businesses (Washington, D.C.: Minority Business Development Agency, September, 1983).

[49]Richard Stevens, "Measuring Minority Business Formation and Failure," (Washington, D.C.: U.S. Department of Commerce, Minority Business Development Agency, December, 1983).

[50]David Birch and Susan McCraken Corporate Evolution: A Micro Based Analysis (Washington, D.C.: Small Business Administration, January, 1981).

[51]Timothy Bates "Profitability in Traditional and Emerging Lines of Black Business Enterprise." Journal of Urban Economics, Vol. 5, 1978: 154-171; also Bates and Bradford, 1979, op. cit.; also Bates, 1983, op. cit.; also Bates and Furino, 1983, op. cit.

[52]Bates and Furino, 1983, op. cit.

[53]Ando and Sickles, op. cit.

[54]Handy and Swinton, 1983, op. cit.; also Handy and Swinton, 1984, op. cit.

[55]David Birch, Susan MacCraken and Maureen Trainer, The Evolution of Minority Business Enterprises (Washington, D.C.: U.S. Department of Commerce, Minority Business Development Agency, December, 1983).

[56]Chen and Steven, op. cit.

[57]Studies commissioned by the Minority Business Development Agency in 1983 include, (i) Ando and Sickles (JACA Corporation, Fort Washington, PA.), op. cit., (ii) Bates, Furino and Wadsworth (Development Through Applied Science, DETAS, San Antonio, TX.) op. cit., (iv) Bearse (Princeton, N.J.), op. cit., (v) Birch, MacCraken and Trainer (Massachusetts Institute of Technology, Cambridge, MA.),

op. cit., and (vi) Handy and Swinton (Southern Center for Studies in Public Policy, Clark College, Atlanta, GA), op. cit.

Chapter IV

[1] Joseph Schumpeter, The Theory of Economic Development: An Inquiry Into Profits, Capital, Interest and the Business Cycle (Cambridge, MA: Harvard University, 1934); also Joseph Schumpeter, Capitalism, Socialism and Democracy (New York: Harper, 3rd edition, 1950).

[2] Frank Knight, Risk, Uncertainty and Profit (New York: Houghton Mifflin, 1921).

[3] Harvey Leibenstein, "Entrepreneurship and Development," American Economic Review, May, 1968, 58(2).

[4] I. M. Kirzner, Competition and Entrepreneurship (Chicago: University of Chicago, 1973).

[5] John Harris, "Entrepreneurship and Economic Development," in Business Enterprise and Economic Change: Essays in Honor of Harold Williamson, edited by Louis Cain and Paul Uselding (Ohio: Kent State University Press, 1973): 141-72.

[6] William Baumol, "Entrepreneurship in Economic Theory," American Economic Review, May, 1968, 58(2).

[7] Nathaniel Leff, "Entrepreneurship and Development: The Problem Revisited," Journal of Economic Literature, March, 1979, 17(1), pp. 46-64.

[8] Lance Davis, et. al. American Economic Growth (New York: Harper and Row, 1972).

[9] Richard Kihlstrom and Jean Laffont, "A General Equilibrium Entrepreneurial Theory of Firm Formation Based on Risk Aversion," Journal of Political Economy, 1979, Vol. 87, No. 41, pp. 714-48.

[10] F.P. Ramsey, "A Mathematical Theory of Saving," Economic Journal, Vol. 38, (December, 1928): 543-559.

[11] R. Dorfman, P.A. Samuelson, and R. Solow, Linear Programming and Economic Analysis (New York: McGraw-Hill, 1958) chp. 12.

[12] Edmond Phelps, Golden Rules of Economic Growth: Studies of Efficient and Optimal Investment (New York, W.W. Norton and Company, 1966): 69 - 103.

[13] Kelvin Lancaster, Mathematical Economics (New York: The Macmillan Company, 1968): 174-183.

[14] Edwin Burmeister and A. Rodney Dobell, Mathematical Theories of Economic Growth (New York: The Macmillan Company, 1970): 363-391.

[15] T.C. Koopmans, "Objectives, Constraints, and Outcomes in Optimal Growth Models," Econometrica 1967, pp. 1-15.

[16] Hywel Jones, An Introduction to Modern Theories of Economic Growth (New York: McGraw-Hill, 1976): 204-226.

[17] M. Kamien and N. Schwartz, Dynamic Optimization: The Calculus of Variations and Optimal Control in Management and Economics (New York: North Holland, 1981).

[18] Kennth Arrow and M. Kurz Public Investment, the Rate of Return, and Optimal Fiscal Policy (Baltimore: The Johns Hopkins Press, 1970)

[19] M. Intriligator, Mathematical Optimization and Economic Theory (Englewood Cliffs: Prentice-Hall, 1971): 408-409.

[20] Martin Baily, "Wages and Employment Under Uncertain Demand," Review of Economic Studies, 41, January, 1974, pp. 37-50.

[21] Costas Azariadis, "Implicit Contracts and Underemployment Equilibria," Journal of Political Economy, 83, December, 1975, pp. 1183-1202.

[22] Kihlstrom and Laffont, op. cit.

[23] George Yip, Barriers to Entry: A Corporate Strategy Perspective (Lexington: D.C. Heath, 1982).

[24] R. E. Caves, J. Shirzi, et. al., "Scale Economies in Statistical Analyses of Market Power," Review of Economics and Statistics, Vol. 63, No. 1, February, 1981.

[25] V. K. Gupta, "Suboptimal Capacity and Its Determinants in Canadian Manufacturing Industires," Review of Economics and Statistics, Vol. 61, No. 4, November, 1979.

[26] Leonard Weiss, "The Survival Technique and Extent of Suboptimal Capacity," Journal of Political Economy, June, 1964.

[27] Douglas Needham, Economic Analysis and Industrial Structure (New York: Holt, Rinehart and Winston, 1969): 97-112.

[28] Gary Becker, The Economics of Discrimination (Chicago: University of Chicago, 1957).

[29] Lester Thurow, Poverty and Discrimination (Washington, D.C.: The Brookings Institution, 1969).

[30] Kenneth Arrow, "Models of Discrimination" in Racial Discrimination in Economic Life, ed. Anthony Pascal (Lexington, MA: Lexington Books, 1972).

[31] Anne Kruger "The Economics of Discrimination," Journal of Political Economcy 71 (October, 1963): 481-486.

[32]Paolo Sylos - Labini, Oligopoly and Technical Progress (Cambridge, MA: Harvard University Press, 1969).

[33]Needham, op. cit., pp. 99-110.

[34]Peter Bearse, An Econometric Analysis at Minority Entrepreneurship (Washington, D.C., Minority Business Development Agency, U.S. Department of Commerce, September, 1983).

Chapter V

[1]The procedure of expressing variables in per unit measures to correct for nonconstant variance in disturbance terms resulting from varying sizes in the dependent variable is well established in the econometric literature. See for instance, P. Rao and R. Miller, Applied Econometrics (Belmont, CA: Wadsworth Publishing Company, 1971): 71-80; G. S. Maddala Econometrics (New York: McGraw-Hill, 1977): 265-68; Wannacott and Wannacott, Econometrics (New York: John Wiley and Sons): 134-136; D. Gujarati, Basic Econometrics (New York: McGraw-Hill, 1978): 195-197; and Kelejian and Oates, Introduction to Econometrics (New York: Harper and Row, 1974): 213-16.

[2]Handy and Swinton found that firm size was positively associated with the growth in the number of black-owned firms with paid employees, but not with black-owned firms without paid employees. See J. Handy and D. Swinton, The Determinants of the Growth of Black-Owned Businesses: A Preliminary Analysis (Washington, D.C.: U.S. Department of Commerce, Minority Business Development Agency, September, 1983).

[3]John Boorman, New Minority-Owned Commercial Banks (Washington, D.C.: Federal Deposit Insurance Corporation, 1973).

[4]Timothy Bates and David Bradford, Financing Black Economic Development (New York: Academic Press, 1979).

[5]EEOC data on black professionals and managers are derived from reports to the Equal Employment Opportunity Commission (EEOC) from all corporations of 100 or more employees by metropolitan area. See the 1978 EEOC Report, Minorities and Women in Private Industry, Vols. 1 and 2 (Washington, D.C.: U.S. Equal Employment Opportunity Commission).

[6]The total number of black professionals and managers by SMSA in 1980 is contained in the Social and Economic Characteristics volume for each state (Washington, D.C.: U.S. Bureau of the Census).

[7]The principal components regression technique that was employed is given in S. Chatterjee and B. Price, Regression Analysis by Example (New York: John Wiley and Sons, 1977): 157-180. The results, using this approach, were unstable because of the nonlinear specification of the black commercial bank loan variable, which was required to correct for heteroscedastic distribution of error terms detected by the Park test. (For a discussion of the Park test see D. Gujarati, Basic Econometrics (New York: McGraw-Hill, 1978): 203-204). Essentially, no method

could be devised to successfully separate the square of the black bank loan variable from the variable itself since this technique requires an orthogonal rotation of the variables. Results differed drastically in terms of both signs and significance levels across several variables when different specifications for the black bank loan variable were attempted under this technique.

[8]Hair, Anderson, Tatham, and Grablowsky, Multivariate Data Analysis (Tulsa: Petroleum Publishing Company, 1979) ch. 6.

[9]S.J. Press, Applied Multivariate Analysis (New York: Holt, Rinehart, and Winston, 1972).

[10]R. Rummel, Applied Factor Analysis (Evanston: Northwestern University Press, 1970),

[11]For a discussion of the utilization of orthogonal rotations in factor analysis to derive independent uncorrelated factors see Cooley and Lohnes, Multivariate Procedures for the Behavioral Sciences (New York: Wiley and Sons, 1971); Hair, Anderson, Tatham and Grablowsky, Multivariate Data Analysis (Tulsa: Petroleum Publishing Company, 1979); J. Kim "Factor Analysis," in Statistical Package for the Social Sciences, edited by Nie, Hull, Jenkins, Steinbrenner and Bent (New York: McGraw-Hill, 1975); and R. Rummel, Applied Factor Analysis (Evanston: Northwestern University Press, 1970).

[12]Paul Worwick, "Canonical Correlation Analysis," in Statistical Package for the Social Sciences, eds. Nie, Hill, Jenkins, Steinbrenner and Bent (New York: McGraw-Hill, 1975): 516.

[13]Hair, Anderson, Tatham, and Grablowsky, op. cit., p. 222 and p. 245.

[14]The latent root criterion is similar to the Kaiser rule in principal component analysis. Essentially this criterion suggests that only unrotated factors with ergenvalues greater than or equal to 1.00 should be retained for further analysis. The disadvantage with including unrotated principal components of factors less than 1.00 is that they have even less discrimination power than the original variables, for which the variances were set equal to 1.00. Kaiser also asserts than if P is the number of variables comprising the analysis, then we can expect that the number of eigenvalues greater than one is approximately 1/3 P. In our case, the thirty-one possible principal components were, in fact, narrowed down to ten factors comprising one varimax orthogonal rotation matrix. See Marascuilo and Levin Multivariate Statistics in the Social Sciences (Monterey, CA: Brooks/Cole Publishing Company, 1983) Chapter 6; and H. F. Kaiser, "The Varimax Criterion for Analytic Rotation in Factor Analysis," Psychometrika, 1958, 23: 197-200.

[15]A sample of studies relying on SBA assisted firms include: Robert Yancy, Federal Government Policy and Black Enterprise (Cambridge, MA: Ballinger Publishing Company, 1974); Timothy Bates "Profitability in Traditional and Emerging Lines of Black Business Enterprise," Journal of Urban Economics (April, 1978); Samuel Doctors and Sharon Lockwood, "New Directions for Minority Enterprise," Law and Contemporary Problems (Winter, 1971); and Timothy Bates, Black Capitalism: A Quantitative Analysis (New York: Praeger Publishers, 1973).

[16]These studies consist of those utilizing private data sources from either the 1969 National Business League Survey, private bank loan data, or a single MESBIC. Such studies include: Robert Edelstein, "Improving the Selection of Credit Risks: An Analysis of A Commercial Bank Minority Lending Program, Journal of Finance (March, 1975); Alfred Osborne and Michael Granfield, "The Potential for Black Capitalism in Perspective," Public Policy, Vol. 24 (Fall, 1976) William Strang, "Minority Economic Development: The Problem of Business Failures," Law and Contemporary Problems, Vol. 36, 1971; Andrew Brimmer and Henry Terrell, "The Economic Potential of Black Capitalism" Public Policy, 19 (Spring, 1971); and Flournoy Coles. An Analysis of Black Entrepreneurship in Seven Urban Areas (Washington, D.C.: The National Business League, 1969).

[17]Studies utilizing the MBDA Financial Research Data Base drawn from minority-owned businesses in the Dun and Bradstreet data file, include: William Scott, Antonio Furino and Eugene Rodriquez, Key Business Ratios for Minority-Owned Businesses (Washington, D.C.: Minority Business Development Agency, 1981); Development Through Applied Science, New Perspectives on Minority Business Development: A Study of Minority Business Potential Using the MBDA Financial Research Data Base (Washington, D.C.: Minority Business Development Agency, August, 1983); and Faith Ando, An Analysis of Growth and Failure Rates of Minority-Owned Businesses (Washington, D.C.: Minority Business Development Agency, September, 1983).

[18]The first study showing the relationship between firm size and failure rates for all firms was conducted by David Birch and Susan McCracken. Corporate Evolution: A Micro-Based Analysis (Washington, D.C.: Small Business Administration, January, 1981). A similar finding is reported by Richard Stevens, "Measuring Minority Business Formation and Failure," (Washington, D.C.: U.S. Department of Commerce, Minority Business Development Agency, 1983).

Chapter VI

[1]The Box-Cox procedure allows us to compare the residual sum of squares of the semi-log regression equation with that of the normal regression equation. The variance of the log Y does not change with units of measurement because log cY = log c + log Y, where log c is a constant. The variance of Y, on the other hand, does change with units of measurement. Consequently, Y must be standardized in such a way that its variance does not change with units of measurement. This allows a direct comparison between the two functional forms to be made.

A transformation that allows such a comparison of the residual sum of squares is $Y* = cY$, where $c = \exp(-\Sigma \log Y/N)$, which is the inverse of the geometric mean. By regressing log $Y*$ and $Y*$, respectively, on the explanatory variables, we can then use a nonparametric test to see whether the difference in the two residual sum of squares is significant. The nonparametric test is defined as $d = (N/2) \left[\log \Sigma e_1^{*2} / \Sigma e_2^{*2} \right]$, where Σe_1^{*2} and Σe_2^{*2} are the residual sums of squares in estimating the two transformed functional forms. The d statistic follows a chi-square distribution with one degree of freedom. In this case, d exceeded the critical value and the two functional forms are not equivalent. (For a discussion of the Box - Cox procedure see P. Rao and R.L. Miller, Applied Econometrics (Wadsworth Publishing Company, 1971): 107-111).

Chapter VII

[1]For a discussion of these points see, Timothy Bates and William Bradford, Financing Black Economic Development (New York: Academic Press, 1979) ch. 9.

[2]Timothy Bates, "Characteristics of Minorities Who are Entering Self-Employment," The Review of Black Political Economy. Vol. 15, no. 2, Fall 1986: 51-71.

[3]Norman Nicholson, Milton Esbitt and Kent Currie, "Performance of Minority Banks in a Recession: The 1973-75 Experience," Baylor Business Studies vol. 12, no. 3, pp. 57-68, August 1981; also John Cole, Alfred Edwards, Earl Hamilton, and Lucy Reuben, "Black Banks: A Survey and Analysis of the Literature," Mimeo, October, 1984: 15-22.

[4]Bates and Bradford, op. cit., ch. 6.

[5]Frank Morris, "Promoting Business Growth Is the Best Way to Create Jobs for Blacks," Point of View (Washington, D.C.: Congressional Black Caucus Foundation Inc.) vol. 2., nos. 1-2, p. 16, Spring/Summer 1985.

[6]Bates and Bradford, op. cit., pp. 104-107.

[7]Michael Days, "Blacks and Business: A Special Report," The Wall Street Journal, February 28, 1985, p. 1.

[8]Morris, op. cit., p. 26.

[9]J. Dominguez, Capital Flows in Minority Areas (Lexington MA: Lexington Books): 85-90; also Bates and Bradford, op. cit., pp. 138-141.

[10]A similar conclusion is discussed in T. Bates, The Nature of the Growth Dynamic in Emerging Lines of Minority Enterprise (Washington, D.C.: Government Printing Office, September, 1983).

BIBLIOGRAPHY

Alexis, Marcus. "The Economic Status of Blacks and Whites." American Economic
Review 68, 2 (May 1978): 179-185.

Ando, F., and Sickles, R. An Analysis of Growth and Failure Rates of Minority-
Owned Businesses. Washington, D.C.: Minority Business Development Agency,
September, 1983).

Arrow, Kenneth and Kurz, M. Public Investment, the Rate of Return, and Optimal
Fiscal Policy. Baltimore: The Johns Hopkins Press, 1970.

Bates, Timothy M. Black Capitalism: A Quantitative Analysis. New York:
Praeger Publishers, 1973.

----------. "An Econometric Analysis of Lending to Black Businesses" Review of
Economics and Statistics, 55, 3 (August 1973): 272-283.

----------. "The Potential of Black Capitalism." Public Policy, 21 (Winter 1973):
135-148.

----------. "Employment Potential of Inner-City Black Enterprise" Review of
Black Political Economy, 4, 4 (Summer 1974).

----------. "Government as Financial Intermediary for Minority Entrepreneurs: An
Evaluation." Journal of Business, 48, 4 (October 1975): 541-557.

----------. "Further Comment: Capital Markets and the Potential of Black
Entrepreneurship." Public Policy, 16, 2 (Summer 1978): 477-479.

----------. "Profitability in Traditional and Emerging Lines of Black Business
Enterprise." Journal of Urban Economics, 5, 154-171 (1978).

----------. Urban Economic Transformation and Minority Business Opportunities.
Unpublished MBDA Research Report, May 1981.

----------. "Effectiveness of the Small Business Administration in Financing
Minority Business." The Review of Black Political Economy, Vol. 11, No. 3,
Spring 1981: 321-36.

----------. The Nature of the Growth Dynamic in Emerging Lines of Minority
Enterprise. Washington, D.C.: Government Printing Office, September,
1983.

----------. "Characteristics of Minorities Who Are Entering Self-Employment."
The Review of Black Political Economy. Vol. 15, no. 2, Fall, 1986.

Bates, Timothy M. and Bradford, William, "Lending Activities of Black-Owned and
Controlled Savings and Loan Associations." Review of Black Political
Economy, 8, 2 (Winter 1978): 202-209.

---------- and Lester, Donald D. "Analysis of a Commercial Bank Minority Lending Program: Comment." Journal of Finance (December 1977): 1783-1789.

---------- and Bradford, William. Financing Black Economic Development. New York: Academic Press, 1979.

----------; Furino, A.; and Wadsworth, R. New Perspectives on Minority Business Development. Development Through Applied Science (Minority Business Development Agency, U.S. Department of Commerce, August, 1983).

Baumol, William. "Entrepreneurship in Economic Theory." American Economic Review. 58,2 (May 1968).

Bearse, Peter. An Econometric Analysis of Minority Entrepreneurship (Washington, D.C.: The Minority Business Development Agency, September, 1983)

Becker, Gary. The Economics of Discrimination. Chicago: University of Chicago Press, 1957.

Bergsman, Joel and Jones, Melvin. Modeling Minority Economic Development. Washington, D.C.: Urban Institute Working Papers, The Urban Institute, 1974.

Birch, David. Job Creation in Cities. Cambridge: MIT Program on Neighborhood and Regional Change, 1980.

Birch, David; MacCraken, S.; and Trainer, M. The Evolution of Minority Business Enterprises. Washington, D.C.: Minority Business Development Agency (MBDA), U.S. Department of Commerce, December, 1983.

---------- and Susan MacCracken, "Corporate Evolution: A Micro Based Analysis." Washington, D.C.: Small Business Administration, January, 1981.

Bobo, B. F., and Osborne, A. E., Emerging Issues in Black Economic Development. Lexington Books, 1976.

Boorman, J. New Minority-Owned Commerical Banks. Washington, D.C.: Federal Deposit Insurance Corporation, 1973.

----------. "The Prospects for Minority-Owned Commercial Banks: A Comparative Performance Analysis." Journal of Bank Research, 7, 253.

----------. The Recent Loan Loss Experience of New Minority-Owned Commercial Banks. Washington, D.C.: Federal Deposit Insurance Corporation. Working Paper No. 74-6.

Bradford, William."Minority Savings and Loan Association: Hypothesis and Test." Journal of Financial and Quantitative Analysis, 13, 3 (September 1978): 533-547.

----------, "Financing Minority Businesses: The Impact and Interaction of Federal Government Programs." Journal of Minority Business Finance, (August 1979).

Bradford, William and Bates, Timothy. "An Evaluation of Alternative Strategies for Expanding the Number of Black-Owned Business." Review of Black Political Economy, 5, 4 (Summer 1975): 376-385.

---------- and Osborne, Alfred E., Jr., "The Entrepreneurship Decision and Black Economic Development." American Economic Review, 66, 2 (May 1976): 316-318.

----------; Osborne, Alfred E.; and Spellman, Lewis J. "The Efficiency and Profitability of Minority Controlled Savings and Loan Associations." Journal of Money, Credit and Banking, 10, 1 (February 1978): 65-74.

Brimmer, Andrew. "The Negro in the National Economy." Race and Poverty, edited by J. H. Kain. Prentice Hall, 1969.

----------."The Black Banks: An Assessment of Performance and Prospects." Journal of Finance, 26, 2 (May 1971): 379-405.

----------. "Recent Developments in Black Banking, 1970-71." The Review of Black Political Economy, Vol. 3, 1972.

----------. "Business Services: A Growth Industry." Black Enterprise, Vol. 6, No. 11, January, 1981.

Brimmer, Andrew and Terrell, Henry S. "The Economic Potential of Black Capitalism." Public Policy, 19 (Spring 1971): 289-328.

Burmeister, Edwin and Dobell, A. Rodney. Mathematical Theories of Economic Growth. New York: The MacMillan Company, 1970.

Caplovitz, David. The Merchants of Harlem. Beverly Hills: Sage Publications, Inc., 1973.

Case, Frederic E. Black Capitalism: Problems in Development. New York: Praeger Publishers, 1972).

Caves, R. E.; Khalilzadek-Shirazi, J., et al., "Scale Economies in Statistical Analyses of Market Power." Review of Economics and Statistics, Vol. 57, No. 2, May 1975.

Chatterjee, S. and Price, B. Regression Analysis by Example. New York: John Wiley and Sons, 1977.

Chen, G.; Hurwitz, N.; Kirchhoff, B.; and Stevens, R. Minority Business Today: Problems and their Causes. Washington, D.C.: Minority Business Development Agency, January, 1982.

---------- and Steven, R. "Minority-Owned Business Problems and Opportunities: A 1983 Update." Washington, D.C.: MBDA, U.S. Department of Commerce, June, 1984.

Cole, J.; Edwards; Hamilton, E.; and Reuben, L. "Black Banks: A Survey and Analysis of the Literature." Chapel Hill, October, 1984. (Mimeographed).

Coles, Flournoy. An Analysis of Black Entrepreneurship in Seven Urban Areas (Washington, D.C.: The National Business League, 1969).

----------. Black Economic Development. Nelson Hall Company, 1975.

Cooley, W.W. and P.R. Lohnes. Multivariate Data Analysis (New York: Wiley, 1971).

Cory, P. E., "A Technique for Obtaining Improved Proxy Estimates of Minimum Optimal Scale." Review of Economics and Statistics, Vo. 63, No. 1, February, 1981.

Cross, Theodore L., "A White Paper on Black Capitalism." Boston: Warren, Gorham and Lamont, Inc., 1971.

----------, Black Capitalism, Strategy for Business in the Ghetto. New York: Atheneum, 1971.

Daniels, Beldan; Hansen Derek, Litvak, Larry "Capital Markets: An Analysis of Empirical Data, Current Federal Interventions and Proposed Innovations." Washington, D.C.: Economic Development Administration, Office of Economic Research: Rept. No. EDA/OER-79/066. Monitor 18.

Davis, Lance, et. al. American Economic Growth. New York: Harper and Row, 1972.

Days, Michael. "Blacks and Business: A Special Report." The Wall Street Journal, February 28, 1985.

Doctors, Samuel. Whatever Happened to Minority Economic Development. Dryden Press, 1974.

Doctors, Samuel and Lockwood, Sharon. "New Directions for Minority Enterprise." Law and Contemporary Problems (Winter, 1971).

----------; Diebin; Allen R.; Irons, Edward D.; and Hunter, William C. "A Pilot Study of the Impact of Minority Banks on their Communities." Review of Black Political Economy, 5, 4 (Summer 1975): 386-403.

---------- and Wokutch, R., "SBA Regional Loan Distribution to Minorities." Review of Black Political Economy, Vol., 11, No. 4, 1982..

Dominquez J. Capital Flows in Minority Areas. Lexington, Mass: Lexington Books, 1976.

Dorfman, Robert; Samuelson, Paul; and Solow, Robert. Linear Programming and Economic Analysis. New York: McGraw -Hill, 1958.

Dunker, Jacob M., and Morton, T. Gregory. "Black-Owned Banks: Issues and Recommendations." California Management Review, XVII, 1. Fall 1974): 78-85.

Edelstein, Robert H. "Improving the Selection of Credit Risk: An Analysis of a Commercial Bank Minority Lending Program." Journal of Finance, 30, 1 (March 1975): 37-55.

----------. "Improving the Selection of Credit Risk: An Analysis of a Commercial Bank Minority Lending Program: Reply." Journal of Finance, 32, 5 (December 1977): 1790-1794.

Fein, Rashi, "An Economic and Social Profile of The Negro American." In The Negro American. edited by T. Parsons and K. Clark. Boston: Beacon Press, 1966.

Foley, Eugene. "The Negro Businessman in Search of a Tradition." In The Negro American. Edited by T. Parsons and K. Clark. Boston: Beacon Press, 1966.

Freeman, Richard. Black Elite. New York: McGraw - Hill, 1976.

Glover, Robert. Minority Business Enterprise in Construction. New York: Praeger, 1977).

Gujarati, D. Basic Econometrics. New York: McGraw Hill, 1978.

Gupta, V. K., "Suboptimal Capacity and Its Determinants in Canadian Manufacturing Industries." Review of Economics and Statistics, Vol. 61, No. 4, November, 1979.

Haddad, William and Pugh, G. Douglas, eds. Black Economic Development, Conference of the American Assembly, Columbia University. Englewood Cliffs: Prentice - Hall, 1969).

Hair, J.F., Anderson, R.E., Tatham, R.L., and Grablowsky, B.J. Multivariate Data Analysis. Tulsa: Petroleum Publishing Company, 1979.

Handy, J.W. and Swinton, D.H. "The Determinants of the Growth of Black-Owned Businesses: A Preliminary Analysis." Review of Black Political Economy. Winter, 1984 Vol. 12 No. 4.

Harris, Abram. The Negro as Capitalist. New York: Negro University Press, 1936).

Harris, J.R. Entrepreneurship and Economic Development. Kent State University Press, 1973.

Hogan, Lloyd. "The Impact of the Current Economic Crisis on Black-Owned Businesses" Review of Black Political Economy, 5, 3 (Spring 1975): 314-321.

Hunter, William, and Sinkey, Joseph. A Socially Optimal Subsidization Model for Inducing Commercial Banks to Participate in Minority Business Development. Athens: University of Georgia, 1980.

Intriligator, Michael. Mathematical Optimization and Economic Theory. Englewood Cliffs: Printice - Hall, 1971.

Irons, Edward D. "Black Banking -- Problems and Prospects." Journal of Finance, 26, 2 (May 1971): 407-425.

----------, "A Positive View of Black Capitalism." Bankers Magazine (Spring 1970).

Jackson Esau and King, Stephanie. "Black Business: Review of Problems and Prospects." Ann Arbor: Bureau of Business Research, University of Michigan, 1972).

Jones, Edward H. Blacks in Business. Grosset and Dunlap, 1971.

Jones, Hywel. An Introduction to Modern Theories of Economic Growth. New York: McGraw - Hill, 1976.

Kamien, M., and Schwartz, N. Dynamic Optimization: The Calculus of Variations and Optimal Control in Management and Economics. New York: North Holland, 1981.

Kaiser, H. "The Varimax Criterion for Analytic Rotation in Factor Analysis." Psychometrika, Vol. 23. 1958.

Kelejian and Oates. Introduction to Econometrics. New York: Harper and Row, 1974.

Kihlstrom, R.E. and J.J. Laffont, "A General Equilibrium Entrepreneurial Theory of Firm Formation Based on Risk Aversion." Journal of Political Economy, 1979, Vol. 87, No. 41.

Kim, J. "Factor Analysis." In Statistical Package for the Social Sciences. Edited by Nie; Hull; Jenkins; Steinbrenner; and Bent. New York: McGraw - Hill, 1975

Kirzner, I.M. Competition and Entrepreneurship. Chicago: University of Chicago, 1973.

Klein, Richard H. "Financial Results of the Small Business Administrations Minority Business Loan Portfolio." University of Michigan Business Review (January 1978): 17-26.

Knight, E. E. and Dorsey, T. "Capital Problems in Minority Business Development: A Critical Analysis." American Economic Review, 66, 2 (May 1976): 328-331.

Knight, Frank. Risk, Uncertainty, and Profit. New York: Houghton Mifflin, 1921.

Kruger, Anne. "The Economics of Discrimination." Journal of Political Economy (October, 1963): 481-486.

Koopmans, T.C. "Objectives, Constraints, and Outcomes in Optimal Growth Models." Econometrica, 1967: 1-15.

Lancaster, Kelvin. Mathematical Economics. New York: The MacMillan Company, 1968.

Leibenstein, Harvey. "Entrepreneurship and Development." American Economic
Review (May 1968) 58(2).

Lee, Roy. The Setting For Black Business Development. New York:
Cornell University, School of Industrial and Labor Relations, 1973.

Levine, Mark. Canonical Analyses and Factor Comparison. New York: Sage
Publications, 1976.

Levitan, S.; Johnson, W.; and Taggart, R. Still A Dream: The Changing Status of
Blacks Since 1960. Cambridge: Harvard University Press, 1975.

Light, Ivan H. Ethnic Enterprise in America: Business and Welfare Among
Chinese, Japanese and Blacks. University of California Press, 1972.

Lowry, James H. and Associates. "A New Strategy for Minority Business
Enterprise Development." Washington, D.C.: Department of Commerce, April
1979, Final report, F1893J4 Contract: A0-A01-78-1327.

Maddala, G.S. Econometrics. New York: McGraw - Hill, 1977.

Marascuilo, L.A. and Levin, J.R. Multivariate Statistics in the Social Scineces.
Montery, CA: Brooks/Cole Publishing Company, 1983.

Markwalder, Don, "The Potential for Black Business. The Review of Black
Political Economy, 3, 1 (Fall 1927): 87-93.

Morris, Frank. "Promoting Business Growth Is the Best Way to Create Jobs
for Blacks." Point of View. Washington, D.C.: Congressional Black
Caucus Foundation, Inc., Vol. 2, nos. 1-2, Spring/Summer, 1985.

Nicholson, N.; Esbitt, M.; and Currie, K. "Performance of Minority Banks
in a Recession: The 1973-75 Experience." Baylor Business Studies,
vol. 12, no.3, August, 1981.

O'Connell, John H. Jr., "Black Capitalism." Review of Black Political Economy.
7, 1 (Fall 1976): 67-84.

Ong, Paul M., "Factors Influencing the Size of the Black Business Community."
The Review of Black Political Economy, Vol. 11, No. 3, Spring 1981: 313-319.

Osbourne, Alfred E. Jr., Granfield, Michael E. "The Potential of Black Capitalism
in Perspective." Public Policy, Vol. No. 24, Issue No. 4. Fall 1976), 529-544.

Phelps, Edmond. Golden Rules of Economic Growth: Studies of Efficient and
Optimal Growth. New York: W.W. Norton and Company, 1966.

Pianco, Dimensions of the Hispanic American Entrepreneurial Experience, May
1981. Unpublished MBDA Research Report.

Press, S.J. Applied Multivariate Analysis. New York: Holt, Rinehart, and
Winston, 1972.

Ratajczak, Rosalinda and Tiller, Jeff, Analysis of the Performance of MBDA Client Firms. Atlanta: Georgia Institute of Technology, June 1980).

Ramsey, Frank. "A Mathematical Theory of Saving." Economic Journal (December, 1928): 543-559.

Rao, P. and Miller, R. Applied Econometrics. Belmont: Wadsworth Publishing Company, 1971.

Rummell, R. Applied Multivariate Analysis. Evanston: Northwestern University Press, 1970.

Schumpeter, Joseph. The Theory of Economic Development: An Inquiry Into Profits, Capital, Credit, Interest and the Business Cycle. Cambridge, MA: Harvard University, 1934.

---------- Capitalism, Socialism, and Democracy. New York: Harper (1942), 1950, 3rd edition.

Scott, Earl P. and Jensin, Janet. "Accessibility to Government Resources for Minority Business Development: A Practicum." Review of Black Political Economy, 7, 1 (Fall 1976): 67-85.

Scott, William D.; Furino, Antonio; and Rodriquez, Eugene. Key Business Ratios for Minoirty-Owned Businesses -- Analysis and Policy Implications, Center for Studies in Business, Economics and Human Resources, College of Business,University of Texas at San Antonio, January 1981.

Seder and Burrell. Getting it Together: Black Businessmen in America. Harcourt Brace Jovanich, 1971).

Smith, James P. "The Improving Economic Status of Black Americans." American Economic Review, 68, 2 (May 1978): 171-178.

Stevens, Richard. "Measuring Minority Business Formation and Failure." Review of Black Political Economy, 12,4 (Spring, 1984).

Stevens, Richard and Hurwitz, Norman. "A Review and Critique of the 1977 Survey of Minority-Owned Enterprises." Washington, D.C.: Minority Business Development Agency, February, 1982.

Strang, William. "Minority Economic Development: The Problem of Business Failures." Law and Contemporary Problems, Vol. 36, 1971.

----------. "The Mix of Black Business: Implications for Growth." Business Horizons 62, 68 (November, 1977),

Summers, Bruce J., and Tucker, James F. "Performance Characteristics of High-Earning Minority Banks." Review of Black Political Economy, 7, 4 (Summer 1977): 344-363.

199

Swinton, D., and Handy, J. The Determinants of Growth of Black-Owned Businesses: A Preliminary Analysis. Washington, D.C.: Minority Business Development Agency, November, 1983.

Thurow, Lester. Poverty and Discrimination. Washington, D.C.: Brookings, 1969.

Troinbetta, William L. "The Black Service Station Franchise." Review of Black Political Economy, 7, 4 (Summer 1977): 364-372.

U.S. Congress, Select Committee on Small Business, Hearing Before the Subcommittee on Minority Small Business Enterprise of the Select Committee on Small Business, House of Representative, Ninety-Second Congress, First Session. Washington, D.C.: Government Printing Office, 1972.

U.S. Congress, Senate Select Committee on Small Business, "Study of Minority Business Enterprise Programs" Washington, D.C.: U.S. Government Printing Office, 1978.

U.S. Small Business Administration. "Minority-Owned Business," Appendix C. In The State of Small Business: A Report to the President. Washington, D.C.: U.S. Government Printing Office, 1983.

U.S. Small Business Administration. "Minority-Owned Business," Appendix B. In The State of Small Business: A Report to the President. Washington, D.C.: U.S. Government Printing Office, 1984.

Venable, Abraham, Building Black Business: An Analysis and a Plan. Earl Graves Pub. Comp., 1972.

Wallich, Henry. "The Negro Economy." Newsweek, 70, 1967.

Walters, A. A., "Production and Cost Functions, " Econometrica, January, 1963.

Wannacott and Wannacott. Econometrics. New York: John Wiley and Sons, 1979.

Weiss, L. W., "The Survival Technique and the Extent of Suboptimal Capacity." Journal of Political Economy, June, 1964.

Wilson, Franklin D. "The Ecology of a Black Business District." Review of Black Political Economy, 5, 4 (Summer 1975): 353-375.

Worwick, Paul "Canonical Correlation Analysis." In Statistical Package for the Social Sciences. Edited by Nie, Hull; Jenkins; Steinbrenner; and Bent. New York: McGraw -Hill, 1975.

Yancy, Robert. Federal Government Policy and Black Enterprise. Ballinger Publishing Comp., 1974.

Young, Harding and Hund, James. "Negro Entrepreneurship in Southern Economic Development." In Black Americans and White Business. Edited by Epstein and Hampton. Encino, California: Dickenson Publishing Co., 1971.